I0150540

A JOURNEY OF RICHES

Develop Your Inner Strength

11 Stories to Inspire you!

A Journey Of Riches - Develop Your Inner Strength

11 Stories to Inspire you! © 2020

Copyright © 2020 John Spender
This work is copyright. Apart from any use as permitted under
the Copyright Act 1968, no part may be reproduced, copied,
scanned, stored in a retrieval system, recorded or transmitted,
in any form or by any means, without the prior permission of the
publisher.

The rights of John Spender to be identified as the primary author
of this work have been asserted by him under the Copyright
Amendment (Moral Rights) Act 2000 Disclaimer.

The author and publishers have used their best efforts in
preparing this book and disclaim liability arising directly and
indirectly, consequential or otherwise, from its contents.

All reasonable efforts have been made to obtain necessary
copyright permissions. Any omissions or errors are
unintentional and will if brought to the attention of the
publishers, be corrected in future impressions and printings.

Published by Motion Media International
Editing: Gwendolyn Parker, Irene Cop and Donna Barclay
Cover Design: Motion Media International
Typesetting & Assembly: Motion Media International
Printing: Amazon and Ingram Sparks

Creator: John Spender - Primary Author
Title: *A Journey Of Riches* - *Develop Your Inner Strength*
ISBN Digital: 978-1-925919-14-1
ISBN Print: 978-1-925919-15-8
Subjects: Self-Help, Motivation/Inspiration and Spirituality.

---❖---

Acknowledgments

Reading and writing is a gift that very few give to themselves. It is such a powerful way to reflect and gain closure from the past; reading and writing is a therapeutic process. The experience raises one's self-esteem, confidence, and awareness of self.

I learned this when I created the first book in the A Journey Of Riches series, which is now one of twenty books with over 200 different co-authors from forty different countries. It's not easy to write about your personal experiences and I honor and respect every one of the authors who have collaborated in the series thus far.

For many of the authors, English is their second language, which is a significant achievement in itself. In creating this anthology of short stories, I have been touched by the amount of generosity, gratitude, and shared energy that this experience has given everyone.

The inspiration for A Journey of Riches, Develop your Inner Strength came from my own experience of settling for less than I truly deserved. Of course, I could not have created this book without the ten other co-authors who all said YES when I asked them to share their insights and wisdom. Just as each chapter in this book makes for inspiring reading, each story represents one chapter in the life of each of the authors, with the chief aim of having you, the reader, living a more inspired life.

I want to thank all the authors for entrusting me with their unique memories, encounters, and wisdom. Thank you for sharing and opening the door to your soul so that others may learn from your experience. May the readers gain confidence from your successes, and also wisdom, from your failures.

I say thank you to my family. I know you are proud of me, seeing how far I have come from that 10-year-old boy who was learning how to read and write at a basic level. Big shout out to my Mom, Robert, Dad, Merril; my brother Adam and his daughter Krystal; my sister Hollie, her partner Brian, my nephew Charlie and niece, Heidi; thank you for your support. Also, kudos to my grandparents, Gran and Pop, who are alive and well, and Ma and Pa, who now rest in peace. They accept me just the way I am with all my travels and adventures around the world.

Thanks to all the team at Motion Media International; you have done an excellent job at editing and collating this book. It was a pleasure working with you on this successful project, and I thank you for your patience in dealing with the various changes and adjustments along the way.

Thank you, the reader, for having the courage to look at your life and how you can improve your future in a fast and rapidly changing world.

Thank you again to my fellow co-authors: Susanne Zavelle, Richard Ayling, Melanie Tan, George Kaponay, Andre Messina, Eric Tan, Dean K Walsh, Alexandra Cousins, Mohammed Hisham Khairul Nasir and Zeina Yazbek.

We would greatly appreciate an honest review on Amazon! This is how we gain more readers to our inspiring book!

With gratitude
John Spender

Praise for A Journey of Riches book series

"The *A Journey of Riches* book series is a great collection of inspiring short stories that will leave you wanting more!"
~ Alex Hoffmann, Network Marketing Guru.

"If you are looking for an inspiring read to get you through any change, this is it!! This book is comprised of many gripping perspectives from a collection of successful international authors with a tone of wisdom to share."
~ Theera Phetmalaigul, Entrepreneur/Investor.

"*A Journey of Riches* is an empowering series that implements two simple words in overcoming life's struggles.

By diving into the meaning of the words "problem" and "challenge," you will find yourself motivated to believe in the triumph of perseverance. With many different authors from all around the world coming together to share various stories of life's trials, you will find yourself drenched in encouragement to push through even the darkest of battles.

The stories are heartfelt personal shares of moving through and transforming challenges into rich life experiences.

The book will move, touch and inspire your spirit to face and overcome any of life's adversities. It is a truly inspirational read. Thank you for being the kind open soul you are, John!!"
~ Casey Plouffe, Seven Figure Network Marketer.

"A must-read for anyone facing major changes or challenges in life right now. This book will give you the courage to move through any struggle with confidence, grace, and ease."
~ Jo-Anne Irwin - Transformational Coach and Best Selling Author.

"I have enjoyed the *Journey of Riches* book series. Each person's story is written from the heart, and everyone's journey is different. We all have a story to tell, and John Spender does an amazing job of finding authors, and combining their stories into uplifting books." ~ Liz Misner Palmer, Foreign Service Officer.

"A timely read as I'm facing a few challenges right now. I like the various insights from the different authors. This book will inspire you to move through any challenge or change that you are experiencing."
~ David Ostrand, Business Owner.

"I've known John Spender for a while now, and I was blessed with an opportunity to be in book four in the series. I know that you will enjoy this new journey like the rest of the books in the series. The collection of stories will assist you with making changes, dealing with challenges, and seeing that transformation is possible for your life." ~ Charlie O' Shea, Entrepreneur.

"*A Journey of Riches* series will draw you in and help you dig deep into your soul. Authors have unbelievable life stories of purpose inside of them. John Spender is dedicated to bringing peace, love, and adventure to the world of his readers! Dive into this series, and you will be transformed!" ~ Jeana Matichak, Author of *Finding Peace*.

"Awesome! Truly inspirational! It is amazing what the human spirit can achieve and overcome! Highly recommended!!"
~ Fabrice Beliard, Australian Business Coach and Best Selling Author.

"*A Journey of Riches* Series is a must-read. It is an empowering collection of inspirational and moving stories full of courage, strength, and heart. Bringing peace and awareness to those lucky enough to read to assist and inspire them on their life journey."
~ Gemma Castiglia, Avalon Healing, Best Selling Author.

"The *A Journey of Riches* book series is an inspirational collection of books that will empower you to take on any challenge or change in life."
~ Kay Newton, Midlife Stress Buster, and Best Selling Author.

"*A Journey of Riches* book series is an inspiring collection of stories, sharing many different ideas and perspectives on how to overcome challenges, deal with change and to make empowering choices in your life. Open the book anywhere and let your mood choose where you need to read. Buy one of the books today; you'll be glad that you did!"
~ Trish Rock, Modern Day Intuitive, Bestselling Author, Speaker, Psychic & Holistic Coach.

"*A Journey of Riches* is another inspiring read. The authors are from all over the world, and each has a unique perspective to share, that will have you thinking differently about your current circumstances in life. An insightful read!"
~ Alexandria Calamel, Success Coach and Best Selling Author.

"The *A Journey of Riches* book series is a collection of real-life stories, which are truly inspiring and give you the confidence that no matter what you are dealing with in your life, there is a light at the end of the tunnel, and a very bright one at that. Totally empowering!"
~ John Abbott, Freedom Entrepreneur.

"An amazing collection of true stories from individuals who have overcome great changes and who have transformed their lives and used their experience to uplift, inspire and support others."
~ Carol Williams, Author-Speaker-Coach.

"You can empower yourself from the power within this book that can help awaken the sleeping giant within you. John has a purpose in life to bring inspiring people together to share their wisdom for the benefit of all who venture deep into this book series. If you are looking for inspiration to be someone special, this book can be your guide."
~ Bill Bilwani, Renowned Melbourne Restaurateur.

"In the *A Journey Of Riches* series, you will catch the impulse to step up, reconsider and settle for only the very best for yourself and those around you. Penned from the heart and with an unflinching drive to make a difference for the good of all, *A Journey Of Riches* series is a must-read."
~ Steve Coleman, author of *Decisions, Decisions! How to Make the Right One Every Time.*

"Do you want to be on top of your game? *A Journey of Riches* is a must-read with breakthrough insights that will help you do just that!"
~ Christopher Chen, Entrepreneur.

"In *A Journey of Riches*, you will find the insight, resources, and tools you need to transform your life. By reading the author's stories, you, too, can be inspired to achieve your greatest accomplishments and what is truly possible for you. Reading this book activates your true potential for transforming your life way beyond what you think is possible. Read it and learn how you, too, can have a magical life." ~ Elaine

Mc Guinness, Bestselling Author of *Unleash Your Authentic Self!*

"If you are looking for an inspiring read, look no further than the *A Journey Of Riches* book series. The books are an inspiring collection of short stories that will encourage you to embrace life even more. I highly recommend you read one of the books today!"
~ Kara Dono, Doula, Healer and Best Selling Author.

"*A Journey of Riches* series is a must-read for anyone seeking to enrich their own lives and gain wisdom through the wonderful stories of personal empowerment & triumphs over life's challenges. I've given several copies to my family, friends, and clients to inspire and support them to step into their greatness. I highly recommend that you read these books, savoring the many 'aha's' and tools you will discover inside."
~ Michele Cempaka, Hypnotherapist, Shaman, Transformational Coach & Reiki Master.

"If you are looking for an inspirational read, look no further than the *A Journey Of Riches* book series. The books are an inspiring and educational collection of short stories from the author's soul that will encourage you to embrace life even more. I've even given them to my clients too so that their journeys inspire them in life for wealth, health and everything else in between. I recommend you make it a priority to read one of the books today!"

~ Goro Gupta, Chief Education Officer, Mortgage Terminator, Property Mentor.

"The *A Journey Of Riches* book series is filled with real-life short stories of heartfelt tribulations turned into uplifting, self-transformation by the power of the human spirit to overcome adversity. The journeys captured in these books will encourage you to embrace life in a whole new way. I highly recommend reading this inspiring anthology series."
~ Chris Drabenstott, Best Selling Author, and Editor.

"There is so much motivational power in the *A Journey of Riches* series!! Each book is a compilation of inspiring, real-life stories by several different authors, which makes the journey feel more relatable and success more attainable. If you are looking for something to move you forward, you'll find it in one (or all) of these books." ~ Cary MacArthur, Personal Empowerment Coach

"I've been fortunate to write with John Spender and now, I call him a friend. *A Journey of Riches* book series features real stories that have inspired me and will inspire you. John has a passion for finding amazing people from all over the world, giving the series a global perspective on relevant subject matters."
~ Mike Campbell, Fat Guy Diary, LLC

"The *A Journey of Riches* series is the reflection of beautiful souls who have discovered the fire within. Each story takes you inside the truth of what truly matters in life. While reading these stories, my heart space expanded to understand that our most significant contribution in this lifetime is to give and receive love. May you also feel inspired as you read this book."
~ Katie Neubaum, Author of *Transformation Calling*.

"*A Journey of Riches* is an inspiring testament that love and gratitude are the secret ingredients to living a happy and fulfilling life. This series is sure to inspire and bless your life in a big way. Truly an inspirational read that is written and created by real people, sharing real-life stories about the power and courage of the human spirit." ~ Jen Valadez, Emotional Intuitive and Best Selling Author

Table of Contents

CHAPTER NINE

CHAPTER TEN

CHAPTER ELEVEN

— ❖ —

Preface

I collated this book and chose this collection of authors to share their experience about how they developed their inner strength. This is to assist you and raise your belief that you too can develop your inner strength and move one-step closer to fulfilling your dreams, and live life on your terms even more.

Like all of us, each author has a unique story and insight to share with you. It just might be the case that one or more of these authors have lived through an experience that is similar to circumstances in your life right now. Their words could be just the words you need to read to help you through your challenges and motivate you to continue on your journey.

Storytelling has been the way humankind has communicated ideas and learning throughout our civilization. While we have become more sophisticated with technology, and living in the modern world is more convenient, there is still much discontent and dissatisfaction with one's reality. Many people have also moved away from reading books, and they are missing valuable information that can help them to move forward in life with a positive outlook.

I think it is essential to turn off the T.V.; to slow down and to read, reflect, and take the time to appreciate everything you have in life.

I like anthology books because they carry many different perspectives and insights on a singular topic. I find that sometimes when I'm reading books that has just one author, I gain an understanding of their viewpoint and writing style very quickly, and the reading becomes predictable. With this book, and all of the books in the *A Journey of Riches* book series, you have many different writing styles and viewpoints that will help shape your perspective towards your current set of circumstances.

Anthology books are also great because you can start from any chapter and gain valuable insight or a nugget of wisdom without the feeling that you have missed something from the earlier episodes.

I love reading many different types of personal development books because learning and personal growth is vital to me. If you are not learning and growing; well, you're staying the same. Everything in the universe is growing, expanding, and changing. If we are not open to different ideas and different ways of thinking and being, then we can become close-minded.

The concept of this book series is to open you up to different ways of perceiving your reality. It is to encourage you and give you many avenues of thinking about the same subject. My wish for you is to feel empowered to make a decision that will best suit you in moving forward with your life. As Albert Einstein said, **"We cannot solve problems with the same level of thinking that created them."**

With Einstein's words in mind, let your mood pick a chapter in the book, or read from the beginning to the end and allow yourself to be guided to find the answers you seek.

If you feel inspired, we would love an honest review on Amazon.

With gratitude,
John Spender

"Failure gave me strength.

Pain was my motivation."

~ Michael Jordon

CHAPTER ONE

❖

Inner Strength Is Your Truth

By John Spender

Limitless

Standing at the gas station filling her car, Jessica became aware of being watched. This made her feel insecure, compounding all of her vulnerabilities on top of each other like cards in a deck. You could hardly blame the young boy sporting a fresh crew cut, probably given by the hands of his father, who was standing right next to him filling his pickup. Most people at this gas station knew Jess; her achievements are well known in these parts. The father and son might have been ranchers from out of town and may well not have known about the local girl.

In the early days, it was hard for Jess to come to terms with her uniqueness. Standing there on one leg and adding gas with the opposite foot wasn't a stretch for Jess. She felt like a normal able-bodied person going about her day-to-day responsibilities. The boy, in awe and never taking his eyes off her, asked his father what happened with the woman. Of course,

Jess, being within earshot, heard everything, and it caused her to shrink even more. Seeing Jessica's discomfort, the father apologized and explained to his son that it's rude to ask such questions. Well and truly rattled, Jess began doing her deep breathing exercises. After these types of incidents, Jess took an hour or two to regain her composure.

Being born with no arms, Jess learned to adapt at an early age; her mother would paste toys to her feet, and her father was adamant that the rest of the family treat her just the same as everyone else. Jessica developed complete dexterity in her toes, almost the same way we use our fingers. I watched, inspired, as she signed a copy of her book *Disarm your Limits* right before my eyes, and her writing was elegant, stylish and neat.

I had come to know Jess through her heroic exploits as the world's first and only armless pilot, flying light aircraft with no modifications, and landing herself a place in the *Guinness World Records* on the 10th of October 2008. Jessica is also a black belt in Taekwondo; plays the piano, cooks, and drives a standard car with no modifications. My team and I were at Jess's place, interviewing her for the movie documentary *Adversity,* which I wrote and produced. As you can imagine, it was an inspiring day for the crew and me. After spending time with Jess, reading her book and watching the film footage again, I gained a deeper understanding of what she lives for;

she just wants to live a rich, full life while expanding in others the belief that anything is possible.

Most people would think that Jess's biggest challenge is having no arms, when, in fact, it's dealing with other people's perception of what she should and shouldn't be able to do in life. Jessica was banned from all rides at Universal Studios Theme Park in Orlando, Florida. The staff handed her a pamphlet stating that riders must be able to "continually grasp," and she couldn't go on the children's rides as they didn't have seat belts.

Fighting for her civil liberties is something Jessica is accustomed to dealing with as she endeavors to live life to the fullest. She has to work harder to get the same results as able-bodied people, mostly because of the limited viewpoint of rule-makers. The average time to get a pilot's license is six months; it took Jessica three years. She had to retake her driver's license when another driver reported her concerns to authorities. However, Jessica has an unrestricted driver's license to this day.

Fighting for your rights to live a full life may have different challenges, but you can be guaranteed that everyone has had their fair share of challenges. By fighting for her rights—and to prove people wrong— Jessica has cultivated incredible determination, inner strength, and high self-esteem. By facing our challenges head-on, we develop the courage, resolve, and mindset needed to succeed beyond our current circumstances. Sometimes it takes someone who doesn't appear to be as blessed as we are to set an example for what's worth fighting for in life.

The limit someone else sets does not have to be the standard we set for ourselves. If Jessica Cox can live a full and productive life with her inner grit and never-say-die attitude, imagine what's possible for the rest of us?

Waking up your Genius

There he was, choking on his vomit after eating the wrong piece of vegetation in the jungles of Hawaii in the pursuit of his passion: big wave surfing. If John DeMartini didn't receive medical attention, he was going to die.

Three years previously, DeMartini had hitchhiked his way from the family home in Houston, Texas, almost 4,000 miles to the North Shore of Oahu, Hawaii. Armed with a small amount of savings and a note of promise stating he wasn't a runaway, the fourteen-year-old DeMartini panhandled and bummed his way across the mainland, and even getting a free ride on a ship for the last leg of his journey. Having struggled with mobility from the beginning of life, DeMartini suffered from a birth defect forcing him to wear hand and leg braces until he was four years old. As he grew and no longer needed the braces, young John took up baseball and various other sports. Moreover, ten years later, he was walking across the country.

At school, DeMartini found it difficult to read and write, and to articulate his thoughts to his peers. Later, he was diagnosed with dyslexia and a speech impediment. In first grade, John's teacher informed his parents that he would never read, write, or communicate; he would not amount to anything nor go very far in life. In the 1960s, a teacher's word was considered gospel, and so the seed was planted in the minds of John's parents to prepare him for a life of manual labor. Because of this, DeMartini's dad encouraged him to be of service and set about teaching him the value of money and fair exchange. His dad had him do chores around the house and, in exchange, the boy would receive pocket money. John's father also encouraged him to start his own lawn mowing and gardening business in their local neighborhood. Young John needed to use his dad's tools and lawnmower, and his dad, wanting to mimic the real world, charged him a small percentage of his earnings as a rental fee. Talk about tough love, right? His father's ways taught John to become independent, enabling him to be self-reliant and to fend for himself at a tender age.

After he'd made his way to Oahu, DeMartini lived off the jungle and begged for necessities for three years while surfing, expanding his consciousness through herbal means, and living in a tent with few possessions. He was living every surfer's dream life.

Strychnine poisoning can be fatal and is commonly used by assassins; in John's case, he simply ate the wrong plant. He was extremely fortunate on that fateful day. This one experience would change the course of DeMartini's life forever. A local medicine woman heard him convulsing. She took him to the nearby health food store and fixed him an antidote to the strychnine. She then invited him to a talk by Paul Bragg, which they were hosting later that night. This was the synchronistic meeting that changed DeMartini's life. Bragg was a speaker, author, and health food advocate whose topics centered around detoxification, dieting, fasting, longevity, natural hygiene, and physical fitness. He awoke the genius inside DeMartini that night, and John was lucky enough to study with Paul for three weeks.

Soon after John returned to the family home in rural Richmond, 40 minutes out of Houston, Texas, he took the G.E.D. test (the General Education Development test, an alternative to a conventional high school diploma) and then the A.C.T. test (college entrance exam) and miraculously passed both of them by guessing and using the affirmation that Paul Bragg gave him. Paul had instructed DeMartini to say this at least 100 times every day to assist with his learning challenges: "I am a genius and I apply my wisdom." If you say something long enough, you start to believe it.

Only after passing both tests was John accepted at Wharton Junior College at age 18. Miserably failing his first test in History, John became discouraged and almost gave up. If it weren't for his mother's love and assistance, he would have quit. DeMartini began to pass his classes and, with an enormous amount of hard work, dedication, and study, he started to excel academically. His peers saw him as a genius who took action towards his dreams, and DeMartini even paid his way through a chiropractic degree by mentoring other students and running group study sessions. After decades of operating a number of his chiropractic centers, DeMartini developed his own educational institute and now travels around the world, teaching his breakthrough programs. Dr. John F. DeMartini is considered a savant by many of his followers to this day.

Like Jessica Cox, John DeMartini had to overcome the perception of people in positions of authority; those who would try dictating the outcome of his life. It must have been hard to hear words of condemnation from his first-grade teacher, especially back in the 60s when it was much harder to challenge the status quo. But, in hindsight, that was the best thing DeMartini's first-grade teacher could have done.

What is the defining moment that gives someone an abundance of inner strength to persevere through the challenges that life throws at him? Could the answer be love, mental conditioning, and adversity? Jessica Cox was raised to use her feet and toes from birth; she had no idea that she was any different from the other children. Her family treated her like an able-bodied person. She was repeatedly conditioned to use her feet and was encouraged to take up sports just like the other kids. The fact that things would be much harder for Jess with the name-calling only strengthened her tenacity to succeed.

When she was nine, Jess's mom would take her to dance lessons after school, and one day they were preparing for a live performance. Jess had become quite shy, mostly from the teasing and bullying by the other children. She was doing well during dance rehearsals, but when it came to the day of the show, Jessica told her mom she was quitting. A little encouragement from her dance teachers convinced her to dance on stage; being so nervous, Jess stared at her feet the entire time, not daring to look at the audience. Jessica's performance received a standing ovation and she stood next her teacher on stage while she received an honorable mention. After that, Jess fell in love with performing.

Dr. John DeMartini's diamond-in-the-rough story emphasizes our love for the underdog; it's a beautiful thing when the odds are stacked against someone and he defeats his adversity. The desire of John's parents to give him a practical education to counterbalance his slow start to life conditioned him to be self-sufficient. From a young age, John's mother would give him small grocery lists and send him to the local store with money. When he returned, they would do the math to make sure John had received the correct change. This practical approach to raising DeMartini prepared him to be able to pay his way through college and to start his chiropractic business. When faced with the challenge of attracting more clients to his practice, John demonstrated initiative by promoting his public talks through a megaphone at the local shopping center, thereby illustrating that inner strength is to be able to face your fears and focus on solutions.

Confront the Fear

I can relate to DeMartini's story in many ways. Growing up as a boy, while I didn't have any physical disabilities, my dad was to be feared and could become physically violent at the drop of a hat. As a result, I developed a lot of uncertainty around thinking for myself for fear of making a mistake resulting in the wrath of my father. Luckily, my parents divorced when I was five. Although it was a confusing time, as I love my dad, I can see now that it was best for my development as a man today.

A slow learner in my early school days, I didn't learn how to read and write until I was ten years old. Miss Day was my saving grace, and she helped my mom to acquire an English tutor for me.

I never went on an epic adventure at a young age, but I caught the travel bug back in 2002, and I have been traveling overseas every year since. My mom helped me to move to Sydney when I was 18 after I enrolled in a horticulture college that allowed me to finish the last two years of high school while I worked toward a degree. After studying my butt off, I topped my class; this highlighted to me that if you want something badly enough you will put in the work. A few years later, I was running a successful landscaping business with 15 employees, while struggling to come to terms with the sexual and physical abuse of my childhood. I turned to drugs (more about this in book nine of the *A Journey of Riches* series *Transformation Calling*.) I sold my last landscaping business almost ten years ago. Now I focus on sharing inspiring books and films with the world. No matter how many times I've been knocked down, something deep within has propelled me forward.

Sometimes the only way to build inner strength is by dying to the old version of ourselves so that our ideal selves can rise like a phoenix out of the ashes. I remember the first time I went to a public speaking contest back in 2012; it was the international speech contest and speech evaluation contest for

Toastmasters International. The international competition has some 30,000 participants from over 140 countries around the world. It's the largest speech contest of its kind, with the winner crowned the world champion of public speaking.

The first round is the club contest. Each club out of 15,900 will hold an international speech contest. The speech is only five to seven minutes long and must be an inspiring personal story. I breezed through the club contest without feeling too nervous, as I was familiar with all of the members. The area contest was a little more challenging, consisting of eight clubs. I had a few nerves, but I felt confident about winning. The speech evaluation began with all of the evaluators listening to a guest speaker and each contestant providing an assessment of what they liked and what could be improved; then concluding with some form of praise. And you only had three and a half minutes to deliver your assessment. I saw public speaking as a healthy challenge.

The only problem at the area contest was that the guest speaker did a terrible job. He stumbled, forgot his lines, and failed miserably. It was tough to find anything positive to say at all. I froze in front of the audience for what seemed an eternity, bowing out with a fizzle.

I had only been a member for two months, so it wasn't a big deal to get knocked out. My main focus was on the international speech contest. I was practicing every day in the weeks leading up to the competition and I knew my speech inside out. I delivered my speech to other clubs and recorded it so I could listen to it on repeat. My presentation shocked people with its intensity and graphic detail of being physically abused as a child. When I shared it with my speaking coach, he asked me if I was sure about delivering this particular speech for the contest. He warned me that a Toastmasters crowd might not be the right audience. Once he understood that I was determined to go ahead, he helped me to refine it.

In the marshaling area, we had to choose a slip of paper to determine the speaking order; lucky for me, I drew number seven. It's good to go towards the end so you can leave a lasting impression on the audience and judges. I enjoy the process of mastering the internal struggle with emotions before going on stage. It's better to allow the nervousness to move through you; I see it as a positive sign and powerful energy to be transformed into a strong and effectivestart to a speech. You just need to remember to keep breathing deliberately.

I delivered the nuances of my remarks to the best of my ability and smoothly progressed to the division contest. This is where the competition goes into another level of skill. There were close to a hundred people in attendance and lots of Toastmaster officials from all over Sydney. I was the second-youngest competitor and the audience was an older crowd. We drew numbers. I was number five, right in the middle and in a much better position than going first. All the speakers sat in the front row by the stage, waiting for the official proceedings to pass before we delivered our speeches. My nerves were out of control; I felt like my heart was going to beat right out of my chest. It reminded me of the time when driving to my very first presentation at Mission Australia. My panic attack almost made me pass out.

As it got closer to my turn to speak, my nerves became worse. I exercised a calming technique that I had developed a few years earlier. When sitting with your nerves becomes too much, four by four breathing can be helpful. You breathe in for four seconds, hold four seconds, breathe out for four seconds, and hold again for four seconds. Repeat until you feel a sense of calm move over you like a small wave gently washing onto the shore. It worked for me, and I was ready when my turn came.

My speech went well from a delivery point of view, but the older audience mostly didn't enjoy it at all. Although I came in second, I received a few messages politely telling me that this kind of speech doesn't belong in Toastmasters. I also had a few people congratulate me, which makes it all the more worthwhile. I had a little laugh to myself about the negativity. Your experiences are your stories and they deserve to be shared. You just never know who you will inspire by being authentic. It was important to me to own my story, and after sharing my emotional pain in a speech, its power over me was released. That memory didn't own or run me anymore. I gained a sense of acceptance and control over my past, and it felt empowering.

As for losing after investing so much effort, I realized that losing isn't to be feared. Losing can mean you are not the biggest fish in the pond, so to speak. Losing is an opportunity to grow. Positive self-talk is another secret weapon to utilize when stretching yourself beyond your usual swimming depth. You can guarantee that Jessica Cox and Dr. John DeMartini have a strong sense of worth and belief in themselves and that their inner dialog is a strong aspect of their faith. DeMartini often states how meaningful affirmations have been to his success: if you say something long enough, you begin to believe it, and before long, you are living it.

Going After What You Want

Jesse Itzler flew across the States to one of the first T.E.D. events in Monterey, California, figuring there would be a lot of high net worth individuals there with money to fly with his jet company. He didn't have a ticket to the event, and he couldn't buy a ticket because it was sold out and most of the seating was by invitation only. Itzler had a unique timeshare idea for travel via private jet. Instead of a five-year membership, he would sell memberships by the hour with a minimum spend of 25 hours. The only thing missing was customers to ride on the jets, and hence Itzler's trip to Monterey.

Asking empowering questions can lead to big ideas. Jesse's jet idea was born when he was invited to fly with the gentleman who bought his jingle company. When he boarded the jet, Itzler was blown away; he couldn't believe that people flew in private jets. Immediately Jesse and his business partner and childhood friend, Kenny Dichter, decided to start a private jet company so they could fly this way a few times a year. Earlier Itzler and Dichter had sold Alphabet City Sports Records to SFX Entertainment for $4 million in stock and cash up front, plus a percentage of future earnings. They had cash to spend.

The plan was to make flying by private jet more affordable for the masses, and this is how they came up with the 25-hour jet card. The next step was finding the jets! The pair considered the shortest route from point A to point B. At the time, there was only one company providing this service and that was Warren Buffet's company, Net Jet, with 650 jets in its fleet. Jesse happened to be owed a favor by Net Jet's then-president, Jim Stewart. Organizing the meeting was no problem, but it only lasted 12 minutes before they were thrown out.

Then C.E.O. Rick Santulli said, "You must be crazy if you think we are going to give two 27-year-olds who probably didn't break a thousand on their S.A.T. scores access to our fleet." Itzler thought they were done, but Jim said they had a shot, because Santulli didn't give anyone 12 minutes. Jim told them to come back the following week. This time they brought their focus group celebrities, like Carl Banks from the New York Giants, the rapper Run from Run D.M.C., and a powerful female real-estate mogul in New York, and they had them to give testimonials stating they would never purchase a five-year membership with Net Jet. But they would buy 25 hours of time a year with Marquis Jet. A deal was done, and they did five billion dollars in sales their first year!

Rewind to the first customer that Jesse Itzler landed for his new company, Marquis Jet. They had access to a fleet of planes but no customers. Not really having a plan and knowing nothing about the aviation industry, Jesse had no playbook for what he should do next. Security for the T.E.D. event was like Fort Knox. He was faced with a problem. Jesse decided to grab a coffee and ponder the situation.

Smelling a sale, a crazy idea popped into his head. He noticed that the participants of the event were coming in and getting a coffee and a muffin. Itzler figured that if he bought all the muffins, the high net worth individuals attending the event would have to get their muffins from him. The next morning Itzler purchased all the muffins and waited outside for people who were eager to have one. As the attendees left the coffee shop disappointed, Jesse Itzler, representing Marquis Jet, greeted them outside the door with free muffins. As a connector that was the perfect conversation starter: "I'm XYZ. Would you like a free muffin?" Then, "By the way, what do you do?" Next minute, he had found himself in a conversation with a guy who was now asking Jesse what he does. It turned out the guy had just sold his company, half.com, to eBay and was looking for a jet service. The man ended up becoming their best customer, and he referred all his friends.

What an incredible story of courage and self-belief. Every time I consider the story, I feel inspired. Inner strength is a muscle, a form of conditioning forged through consistency that creates a blueprint of neuro-pathways in your brain, enabling you to do something again and again. Jessica was conditioned from a young age to believe she was no different from her siblings and, still, life would push back. She developed an I'll-show-you attitude, and is now a successful motivational speaker traveling to more than 20 countries sharing her message of Life Without Limits.

When his friends were going to college, Itzler was writing rap songs and scored a contract with Delicious Records. He was sacked a year later, but that led him to writing and singing the theme jingle

for the New York Knicks NBA team—*"Go* **NY** *Go"*—
which went on to become a huge hit. This was a
reminder that he could achieve anything in life, and
he formed his first million-dollar company, Alphabet
City Sports Records.

Jesse's parents had allowed him to explore life within
reason, and a defining moment in his youth was when
his sister drove him and a friend from their home in
Long Island to D.C. This was the era of break dancing
and Jesse and his friend were quite good. The idea
was that they would do a street performance and ask
for money in Washington Square. At the end of the
day, they had made 200-odd dollars, not bad for two
14-year-olds. They felt rich! On the drive up, Itzler
had been so nervous he could hardly breathe. Crazy
thoughts had been running through his head like,
What if we suck and people start bagging us out? Or,
Am I up to showcasing my talents? We all know those
random thoughts of self-doubt that appear any time
we step outside of our known realities.

This first real win in Jesse's life set the tone for the
rest. It became a reference point to look back on
whenever he needed to take a chance on himself.
Sometimes it takes someone else to awaken that
special something inside you, like that night when
Paul Bragg awoke DeMartini's genius. John went from
thinking he wasn't intelligent to believing he could go
to college and live a successful life. It's strength to
have a peer group that believes in your dreams. We

are the average of the five people we associate most closely with in our day-to-day lives.

It's a beautiful thing that more and more people around the world are seeing the strength of expressing their emotions from a place of vulnerability. Public speaking was the outlet that helped me to express myself from a place of vulnerability. I used to be terrified of sharing or speaking up in public. Sometimes, though, it's the right time to dig deep and find your courage. Toastmasters was the main outlet for me where I could bare all. Mission Australia was another, and I also use to host my own events. With the latter, the biggest fear was that no one would show up. I would hand out event flyers at the train station near the venue, email everyone I knew, and do social media posts. All that for 30 people to show up! I had a little success in Singapore and had 85 people attend one of my events at The Hub. It was a lot of effort though.

It does get easier to manage your nerves, and it's so rewarding to break through your fears and strengthen your self-belief. Once you develop the skill of public speaking, it's like riding a bike: the ability never completely leaves you. Contrary to public speaking, though, I'm still working on the vulnerability that comes with one-on-one communication. It's still challenging for me to express how I'm really feeling with a woman when I'm dating. It's like my vulnerability brings up my past traumas and my heart naturally wants to close. I've been learning to be more open to how I'm feeling and to really move through whatever emotion is present and to really feel it rather than to ignore it altogether or distract myself with my phone, or get defensive. The reaction would depend on the situation, but these are my go-to strategies of escapism.

A tremendous help in conquering the personal communication challenges has been the men's circle near where I live in Ubud, Bali. I started attending last year, but it's only been recent that I've gone a few weeks in a row. At first, I found it very intimating to sit with a group of men and share how I was truly feeling in the present moment with none of my go-to defenses at hand. It's a feeling of complete exposure, but at the same time, it's liberating to be seen and to receive a nod of recognition by someone within the circle who might also be going through something similar to my situation. It's comforting to know that we are not alone in our struggles; there is a lot of strength in solidarity.

It's humbling to accept that we don't always have to have a solution to every difficulty that we might be facing. Sometimes it's enough to be heard and acknowledged, to know that we don't go through our challenges alone. All we need is the courage and support to express how we are feeling. Inner strength isn't just about continuing through difficult times or taking risks to expand your reality or to fulfill your dream. By facing different aspects of ourselves, we can personally strengthen our sense of self. This helps us to create a stronger relationship with ourselves.

It doesn't matter what other people think if you have a belief in your ability. For instance, Jessica didn't believe that she was limited, but she had to overcome the idea that she was handicapped, an idea that the general public projected on her. Her spirit within was stronger than public opinion. Dr. Demartini learned that he was smart, regardless of what his teacher wanted him to think of himself. Jesse reached inside for the talent to open up a world of success for himself, and the sky was the limit. And I am learning to speak for the abused child that I once was. The struggle is real, but so is the strength. The power is within, and awaking to that inner strength is the truth we seek.

"Strength is not born from strength. Strength can be born only from weakness. So be glad for your weakness's now; they are the beginning of your strength."

~ Claire Weekes

CHAPTER TWO

❖

Receiving More by Letting Go!

By Susanne Zavelle

Everyone has a story that can either strengthen or destroy him.

I believe that everything happens for our ULTIMATE good, even those moments of despair and darkness that threaten to overwhelm us.

As you read my story, you will be inspired to dig deep, stay positive, and ultimately feel tremendously hopeful for this moment and the future. You will come to see how thoughts become things, and how controlling your mind is paramount to success in every area of life.

The Back Story

Growing up on a 2,000-acre ranch in Texas gave me a childhood that very few ever get to experience. It was like *Little House on the Prairie*, complete with a well from which to draw water, a wood-burning stove, and an outhouse. While we weren't poor, my grandfather lived through the Great Depression, and he carried the scars. We learned to ride horses before we could walk, and every spring, I looked forward to rounding up the cattle.

We spent weekends, holidays, and summers on the ranch, and the rest of the time, we lived in Austin. One of the first memories I have as a young girl was sitting on the tailgate of my dad's truck, looking out over the vast landscape, watching the cattle and listening to the horses whinnying in the background. He said, "Someday, all of this will be for you and your kids and grandkids. You will never have to worry about money because, when I'm gone, you'll be a multi-millionaire." My father was a criminal defense attorney, and he did very well in the stock market. I didn't understand what all of that meant, but it was still a pivotal moment for me.

Sadly, my father's alcoholism consumed my parents' marriage and my parents divorced. My father and I had a very tumultuous relationship. Like any young girl, I craved the attention and praise of my dad and he couldn't give that to me. Later, I came to understand that you can only give someone what you already have. From the little I know about his upbringing, I don't believe my father ever felt loved as a child. Therefore, he didn't know how to show it himself. I know that now, but as a young girl and young adult, it was crushing to hear drunken rages, name-calling, and threats of being "cut off."

My dad had a twisted way of using money, and the threat of being disowned by him kept me in line for the majority of my adult life. His harsh words and threats held me captive to thoughts of not being good enough to make it on my own. As a result, I made some poor relationship choices.

I had two failed marriages by the time I was 23. I had basically married my father each time. I was looking for a knight in shining armor to rescue me, and I was completely unaware that my thinking and mindset had put me and kept me in a place of continually repeating history.

When I was 24, I met a man who I would eventually marry and have two beautiful children with. He was in medical school, and I was in nursing school. He came from a wonderful family, was a Harvard graduate, and we were so in love. We married in 1996 and had two sons within four years. Life was good!

The Challenge

Suddenly, our dream life came crashing down. We had taken financial advice from accountants and attorneys who turned out to be crooked. Over 2,000 hard-working American families got caught up in the scam. We were young, naïve, and didn't do our due diligence.

The investments were called into question by the U.S. Government. Federal agents showed up at our front door one day in 2001. At the time, we still believed that the investments were legitimate.

How foolish we were back then! We refused to believe that we had been taken advantage of. Later we learned that almost $300,000 was stolen from us in a Ponzi scheme, but at the time, we were clueless and in total denial. The mind is a powerful thing!

The following year, the same agents came back to our house. This time my husband made a mistake. He would regret it for the rest of his life. He called the agent "a messenger boy" and essentially sealed our fate with a single outburst of anger. Two weeks later, in what our attorneys called "nothing but retaliation," our home was raided at gunpoint by ten federal agents in front of our little boys, aged two and four. They stormed in as if we were drug traffickers, turning our home upside-down and severely traumatizing us.

I felt so hopeless and afraid. The fact that we had made such a foolhardy mistake, one that could potentially lead to prison time, was beyond comprehension. My thoughts raced obsessively: my husband going to prison, me going to prison... being separated from my children... the embarrassment of making such a foolish mistake... the disappointment of my father and the rest of my family...on and on. I couldn't make them stop.

The depression and anxiety were so severe that I lost almost 20 pounds in two weeks, and I was already skinny. The cloud over my head was so dark, so overwhelming that I couldn't sleep, couldn't eat, and could not focus on ANYTHING other than this.

We were under a Federal investigation.

My former life, dreams, hopes, plans, and feelings of safety were obliterated in a matter of hours. The raid was always there in the back of my mind. I was constantly reliving the event in my dreams and my daily life. Every time there was a simple knock on the door, my heart would pound and flutter in my chest. I felt an overwhelming sense of edginess and apprehension. I had post-traumatic stress syndrome.

"Unlike simple stress, trauma changes your view of your life and yourself. It shatters your most basic assumptions about yourself and your world — "Life is good," "I'm safe," "People are kind," "I can trust others," "The future is likely to be good" — and replaces them with feelings like "The world is dangerous," "I can't win," "I can't trust other people," or "There's no hope."

~Mark Goulston MD,
Post-Traumatic Stress Disorder for Dummies

Suicide is seen as selfish to outsiders looking in, but when I was in the middle of the nightmare, I couldn't think, much less rationally, about the potential effects of me not being there for my children and others who loved me. When I was in that state of obsessive thinking, I couldn't see any other way out.

I didn't want to DIE; I just wanted the madness, the pain, the uncertainty to end. I felt like the world was caving in on me. I wanted out, and one night I got out my husband's toxicology book to figure out how to make that happen. Strange… I was mentally sound enough to calculate a fatal dose but irrationally figured my kids would be okay because, after all, my husband was off work the next day. My mind was not right!

The first thing I heard on waking up were the sounds of my husband wailing and crying as he desperately worked to save my life. The night before, I had written a suicide note before ingesting twice the lethal dose of Tylenol, along with a bottle of Xanax, which had been prescribed for the unbearable anxiety and unrelenting nightmares. I had asked him to sleep in the guest room that night so that by the time he found me I would be gone.

He was the one who found me naked, covered in vomit, and barely alive. He was doing a sternal rub to try to get me to respond. I could hear him and feel him, but I couldn't make a sound. I lost consciousness again. My next memory was of the emergency department physician telling my husband, "She's not going to make it," and then my husband admonishing him and telling him, "You don't know my God. He will save her, and my wife will NOT die!"

After a week-long stay in the Intensive Care Unit, I was released to a psychiatric hospital. They found a good medication for me and taught me how to cope. A week later, I was discharged home. However, life would never be the same.

I will never forget coming home that night. My children were sound asleep. I didn't want to wake them, but I couldn't wait to hold them, either. I was so grateful to be home and among the living. I literally fell on my knees by their little beds and thanked God that I was ALIVE!

I could not believe what I had done. I was overwhelmed with love and gratitude for my family, but with a tremendous amount of guilt and shame over my actions. I had to regroup and prepare for the battle ahead. I had to learn to deal with the ongoing stress because we were told that the investigation could take years.

> **"Trauma destroys the fabric of time. In normal time, you move from one moment to the next, sunrise to sunset, birth to death. After trauma, you may move in circles, find yourself being sucked back into an eddy, or bouncing like a rubber ball from now to then to back again. ... In the traumatic universe, the basic laws of matter are suspended: ceiling fans can be helicopters, car exhaust can be mustard gas."**
>
> *The Evil Hours: A Biography of Post-Traumatic Stress Disorder*
>
> ~David J. Morris

And it did. It took years to get through the whole ordeal. At one point, we received a Victim Impact Letter from the Department of Justice. For a brief moment, we hoped that perhaps they were going to see the truth: we never intended to break the law and put our young family at risk!

They wanted our statements for sentencing the criminals who stole millions of dollars from people like us. I remember thinking, "I could write a movie script about how this has affected me, and you want me to write it on a single sheet of paper?" Sadly, this was the first publicly recognized time in U.S. history that the government then chose to prosecute the victims of fraud. Out of approximately 2,000 people who had been defrauded, 13 of them were slated for prosecution. They needed to make an example out of someone, and we were on the list. It made no sense, but there was nothing we could do about it.

It wasn't until 2008 that the indictment was handed down, a week before the statute of limitations ended. For seven long years, we lived with tremendous uncertainty about the future. Life went on and we coped with the situation as best we could with the tools we had at the time. However, the constant stress and financial drain (over 1.5 million dollars) of legal bills took its toll. Ultimately, in 2009, my husband took a plea deal to spare me of the stress of a trial and the risk of going to prison and being separated from my kids. It was the most self-sacrificing thing that any man could do to protect his wife and take the fall alone.

It would be another five years for us to get back on our feet, and during those five years, he would serve two years of house arrest, five years' probation, and pay back $250,000 that we owed the government. Sadly, due to the plea deal, he lost his ability to work as a physician for almost four years. What do you do when you are a doctor but you can't work as one? We had to get creative, but somehow, by the grace of God, we survived. Fortunately, we didn't lose our home and we narrowly avoided bankruptcy. By the end, it was a 15-year struggle from the beginning of the investigation until we paid back the last cent that we owed. Talk about a drain on your body and mind!

> **"Strength does not come from winning.**
> **Your struggles develop your strengths.**
> **When you go through hardships and**
> **decide not to surrender, that is**
> **strength."**

~ Arnold Schwarzenegger

In time, life went on and eventually returned to normal. My husband returned to practicing medicine. I tried to figure out who I was, because I honestly had no idea. My identity was wrapped up in other people: a wife, a sister, a mother, a friend, a daughter, and a retired Registered Nurse. But *who* was I on the inside? I had no clue.

Having close friends who stick by you through thick and thin is a tremendous blessing. One of my closest lifelong friends was Tinsley. Any time I needed her, she was there for me. We were inseparable!

Then, in 2009, Tinsley was diagnosed with advanced breast cancer. It was a devastating blow for her. She fought a very tough battle, and I was by her side throughout. She had never married or had kids, so I spent a lot of time traveling to be with her during chemo treatments. It was the hardest thing in the world to see my best friend deteriorate.

By 2012, she had no more fight in her. I was by her side at the end. We spent hours upon hours laughing at the memories of so many good times and crying because we knew we would never see each other again on this side of heaven.

Tinsley had a brilliant way with words. Toward the end of her battle, she reached over, took my hand, and said, "Look at me, Sue." I knew she was about to say something serious.

"You don't even know who you are. You have no idea. But I see something amazing in you, and my wish and prayer for you are that you will tap into your power, become who God created you to be, and make a tremendous impact on the world when I'm gone." To say I was shocked is an understatement.

She was right. I didn't have a clue who I was, what I wanted in life, or how to get there. Without vision, you will perish...and I felt like I was perishing.

I had no direction, no real identity apart from other people, and I knew that I had to dig deep and search for answers. Right then and there, I gave her my word that I would discover who I was and tap into my potential; grow myself, and make a positive impact in the world. I would live the rest of my life in such a way that would bring honor to her name and her memory.

It was a promise that would have lasting and far-reaching implications. Tinsley passed on a couple of weeks later. I was left without my best friend. I felt broken and hollow, and yet I had a sense of knowingness that God would show me what to do, and which direction to take.

About six months later, I was at the gym working out and a friend asked me if I had ever considered competing. I looked at him as if he had three heads and said, "No way could I do that!" It was out of the question! I was 46, the mom of two teenagers, and had never trained at that level of intensity.

Later that night, I had what I would call an epiphany. When I was a teenager, I *did* want to compete. I had always admired Rachel McLish, the first Ms. Olympia. She was all-natural and had an amazing physique.

When I was young, I read every article she wrote and even had her poster on my bedroom wall.

I wished I could do something like that – push myself to the limit just to see what my body could do. And then, all at once, waves of deeply seated grief and regret poured out. I wailed as I was brought to my knees with overwhelming feelings of sadness and remorse. I cried as I had never cried before at the clear realization that I—no one else—was responsible for never having chased that dream. I couldn't blame my lack of action or ambition on anyone but myself. I was 100% responsible.

The Decision

"The most difficult thing is the decision to act; the rest is merely tenacity. The fears are paper tigers. You can do anything you decide to do. You can act to change and control your life; and the procedure, the process is its own reward."

~ Amelia Earhart

I knew right then and there that I would compete for Tinsley and myself. It was the beginning of my metamorphosis. I had no idea that this one decision would be the catalyst for so many other changes in my life. It was the beginning of a whole new me.

My husband came home from work that night to find me in a heap on the floor of our bedroom. I was a mess. By the looks of me, he thought someone had died or something. Through the tears, I told him what I had to do. I was going to become a professional athlete. He was taken aback, but he never questioned my decision. He supported me 100%.

I began the process of transforming my frail, thin body. I started an extremely rigorous process of training up to two or three hours per day, six days a week, weighing and measuring my food, and visualizing my results. I would later learn that visualization is a potent tool if done correctly, but at the time, nobody told me how to do it.

I just did what came naturally. I spent ten minutes, morning and night, visualizing my body morphing into a completely different one; my muscles were growing, body fat reducing, and energy increasing. I envisioned the national stage, even though I had no idea of what the stage would look like in person, since I had never attended a bodybuilding competition before. This visualizing proved to be a powerful tool in my arsenal of learning to manifest my dreams. Additionally, I started using an excellent brand of high protein that was being marketed via multi-level marketing; a method I never dreamed would be profitable or appealing to me.

I told my dad what I was doing via email. My first show was only three months away, and I wanted him to attend. Looking back, I can acknowledge that deep down inside, I was still looking for his love and acceptance. All I ever wanted was to make my dad proud of me, especially after feeling like a total failure on a financial level. I was looking for external validation.

About two weeks before my first show, my dad called me. I thought he was going to tell me how excited he was for me. I thought he would be proud of me for chasing my dreams. I was wrong.

Instead, I received an earful of contempt. He lit into me like a fire raging through a drought-laden landscape. It felt like an inferno in my stomach as he proceeded to try to rip apart my dreams.

"Who do you think you are?! What kind of *mother* of two teenage boys gets in a *bikini* on a *stage*? That is the *dumbest*, most *ridiculous* thing I have *ever* heard of in my *life*! You are way too old for this! Why don't you focus on rebuilding your life instead of wasting time on this ludicrous idea? Professional athlete? You can't do that! That's impossible! That is the craziest idea I've ever heard of!"

I was so hurt. Words cannot begin to describe the deep anguish I felt in my soul and my heart. But it didn't stop there. The old habit he had of threatening me with money and intimidating me about being disowned came back, with a vengeance.

"If you do this competition, I am seriously going to have to rethink my estate planning, because you sound psychologically unstable to me!"

It had been many years since he had spoken to me like that. However, I was no longer the marionette waiting for the puppet master to pull my strings. And for the first time in my life, I had the strength to stand up to his bullying. I had made a promise to my best friend on her deathbed, and there was no going back.

I stood firm. With all the courage I could muster and the strength of Tinsley's memory fresh in my heart, I boldly replied, "Dad, you do what you have to do to make you feel better about yourself. If that means disowning me, then so be it. Go ahead and get in your car, go to your attorney's office, and change your damn will, because I'm not for sale and my dreams aren't for sale." And with that, I hung up the phone.

I cried like a baby after that call. I cried for the years of hurt he had caused; for the years I hadn't stood up to him, and for the reality that my kids barely even knew him at all. I cried over the fact that I had never felt loved or accepted; or good enough, smart enough, successful enough, or just *enough*, period. It felt like the weight of the world had been lifted off my shoulders. Yet, I realized that I had just released the only safety net I had ever known in my life. I knew that now it was up to me. So, I got to work!

The Battle Begins

As my body began to reshape itself, people naturally wanted to know what and how I was eating, so it was easy to recommend the network-marketing nutrition products that I was using. I started to bring in a nice monthly paycheck, and that got me thinking: what if this business model works? I learned the skills of network marketing and threw myself deeply into personal growth and development.

I took a program by Rod Hairston, founder of Growth-U. I learned how the mind works, how thoughts are energetic and how we attract people and circumstances that are in line with our frequency of vibration. I dove into studying the Law of Attraction, the Law of Vibration, the Law of Focus, and many of the other Universal Laws. I was a sponge, and I loved the new me that I was becoming.

Meanwhile, within one year of starting, I made it to second place in the nation at the National Physique Committee (NPC) in the over 45 master's Bikini. The national-level stage ended up being exactly how I had visualized it would be! I was becoming a new person with a new identity.

I created a vision board and started visualizing and feeling the experiences as if they were happening in the *now*. One by one, I was manifesting my dreams. I was invited to be an official athlete for my nutritional company and even competed at the Arnold Classic; something I'd never imagined in my wildest dreams. I had created a six-figure income in a matter of a couple of years, and life was so good!

Full Circle

Although I missed my dad, I didn't miss the verbal abuse or threats of being disowned.

In late 2015, my father called. He sounded like an older man. He wanted to know how I was, and I didn't know where to start.

I felt like I had accomplished more in the last three years than I had in my whole life. As I ran through my list of achievements, I could tell that he was sorrowful. He had missed everything, by his own choice. So much had happened and I wasn't the same person. Although he didn't apologize, I could tell in his voice that he regretted his actions. I forgave him immediately. We started to talk every day, and we never had another disagreement.

Meanwhile, my 20-year marriage was crumbling. The stress and financial strain had taken its toll, and it was unbearable for both of us. Over the years, we had tried various counseling methods, but nothing seemed to work. Finally, my husband and I separated, although we remain friends to this day.

A few months later, I took my 18-year-old son skydiving. It was such a thrill! When I landed on the ground, I tried several times to call my father and tell him what we had just done. Finally, the next day, my stepmother answered his phone. She bitterly said to me that he had gotten drunk the night before, fallen, and hit his head. Now he was in the hospital. I was shocked that she hadn't notified me yet! My dad and I had just talked a couple of hours before the accident.

My stepmother insisted that I need NOT come; that he would be fine but would need to go to rehab after he was discharged. I was very concerned. I called every day, and she repeatedly told me that he would be fine and I need NOT to come.

The annual event with my network marketing company was days away. I was scheduled to be on stage in front of 15,000 people, and I wasn't sure if I should even go at that point. My stepmother insisted that I go. Reluctantly, I boarded the plane to Las Vegas.

As I walked down the airplane aisle, I received a text from my half-brother. It said, "We have decided to make dad DNR [Do Not Resuscitate]." I thought it was a joke, but I soon realized that a massive betrayal of the worst kind had happened to me. I would later learn that my sister and brother had been called to my father's bedside, along with his close friends, because he was NEVER going to go home. He was essentially brain-dead and had been since the fall almost two weeks prior.

Tears streamed down my face as I realized what had just happened. He was gone now, and I had to come to terms with that.

I truly believe that God is always on our side. Because I was on that flight and not on my way to Texas, I met none other than Rod Hairston, founder of Growth-U, the personal development company that had changed my life. We talked the whole way to Vegas. Eventually, we became friends and even business partners. Who would have thought?

Being mentored by Rod, a man who has coached many people from zero to billionaire status, proved to be exactly what I needed! My life made a complete turnaround after that chance encounter. He taught me all about mindset, identity, purpose, vision, and how to manifest exactly what you truly desire in life.

> **"Focus on growing and expanding instead of fearfully staying in your comfort zone. Focus on abundance instead of scarcity. Focus on what is right with your life instead of what is**

wrong. When you do that, you'll give energy to the things you want in your life, which will help manifest them. "

~ Rod Hairston, *Are You Up for the Challenge?*

And that is precisely what I did. I began the hard work of peeling the layers back on my soul. I had a lot of work to do!

Anytime I felt fear, I replaced that thought with something positive. I started meditating every day and learned how to do transcendental meditation. I was meticulous about what I focused on: my future. I got VERY clear on exactly what I desired without putting an emotional attachment on HOW I would manifest these things. The vision was manifesting even when I didn't see it.

Now, my life looks completely different! In 2018, I joined a new network marketing company and hit the ground running. Within three months, I hit the top rank and was leading a massive team. Soon after, I chanced upon a couple of start-up companies who needed investment capital. Those companies are on track to explode in earnings! Next, Rod invited me to come on board with his company as they set to expand globally. How could I say no? I went from a net worth of $5000 to becoming a multi-millionaire in a matter of a year. My visions were becoming a reality.

I tell you this not to impress you, but to show you that nothing stays the same. If you are in the middle of a battle, just know that it won't last forever. I have learned some incredible life lessons through all the ups and downs. When you are in the middle of a storm, stop focusing on the problem at hand and, instead, train your mind to focus on the life you desire. You will attract who you ARE, so BECOME that today in your mind. Walk, talk, and think like the person you ultimately want to be. Make sure you spend ten minutes twice per day visualizing and feeling the emotions of reaching your ultimate goals. I was a multimillionaire in my mind long before I actually became one.

Always focus on the positive attributes of your partner because, by focusing on the negative, you will get more of that. I fully recognize that my negative mindset contributed to the demise of my 23-year marriage. Surround yourself with positivity as much as possible and avoid negative people as much as you can. Always remember that these life lessons are not designed to break you, but rather to mold you into the person you were designed to be, and your heartache and journey may just give someone else hope when they are facing a similar challenge.

You can't enjoy or appreciate the mountaintop moments unless you have been in the valley. Embrace the journey and be patient.

"I like to use the hard times in the past to motivate me today."

~ Dwayne Johnston

CHAPTER THREE

❖

Wings not Weights

By Dean K Walsh

"But the new forest that grows back in a scarred heart is sometimes wilder and stronger than it was before the fire."

The Mountain Shadow
~ Gregory David Roberts

There have been times recently when I've heard strange noises coming from me while sitting on the end of my bed with my head in my hands. Tears were dropping on the tiled floor while I glanced sideways at the expensive framed family photos featuring the elated faces of my dear infant children in my arms—pictures that should have been hanging proudly on the wall of my family home in Bali as my wife showered and my kids played with our pet rabbit. This collection of images should feature my stunningly beautiful wife, but those have been excluded and packed away under the stairs, but not cast out in the rubbish for reasons I don't understand. Perhaps there's a chance that one day we can reunite. The thought of that scenario has only added confusion and torment to what's happened in my whirlwind of emotions, disputes, and mental restructuring.

A few minutes pass and I regroup, take a deep breath, and sit up straight to wipe my wet face. I look at myself in the mirror, curious how I appear, as it's only a handful of times in my life that I've wailed like that. I'm aware that if I don't navigate the next few months carefully, utilising what I've learned about pain, I could very well become a broken man relying on destructive decisions that will lead me to complete demise. The magnitude of the love I had for this woman was immeasurable.

I begged my ex-wife to stick with me and see it through—to allow the difficult times to become our stories of triumph one day, making us stronger for having won over whatever it was that we were wading through at the time. I begged her to consider the situations (that she couldn't understand from my angle) in the interest of our dear young children. What would they say to her when they were old enough to speak of the issue at hand: the potential divorce? What would their desires be? I role-played with my wife, paraphrasing the obvious responses from my children as if they pleaded with Mummy and Daddy not to be silly, saying that we love each other, and we won't ever part ways.

Even as I'm writing this, my eyes are wet with the thought of my little darlings having to understand one day that their world is not what it seems, that their world has split into two. That reality is my greatest challenge, which is causing a pain that could (if I weren't strong enough) keep me in bed with the curtains shut for months on end.

My heart breaks. I should be close to them to keep them safe, to teach my son to be a young gentleman and my daughter that she's always safe under daddy's wing and that they can do anything. I attempt to do this now, over the phone, twice a week while pretending we are truly connected and that the experience on Facebook Messenger is fulfilling for both of them and myself.

I focus only on the seemingly positive: that is, I can fly back to Australia to embrace them and be the dad on school holidays. That's all I have to hold on to before I see them again. It'll have to do. I imagine their arms around me when I wake up in the morning here. I see their sweet faces every time I blink throughout the day, and I flinch every time I hear a young child laugh or cry. Something deep within me is innately aware of my loss, which arouses my consciousness to continually search for and expect them in my every waking momont while my old behaviour patterns sit ringside in my mind tormenting me with ideas of how to escape the sadness.

I recall one time during the aftermath, when I visualised a young woman peacefully sleeping in my bed actually being my infant daughter snuggling into my chest, resting blissfully, feeling my love and adoration. Society's false understanding that a mother hurts more than a father when separated from their children is monumentally inaccurate.

I now understand why many men fall when they split from their wives and can't see their children, when the ex spreads unforgivable lies to turn their own friends, whom they love dearly, against them. What's so special about me? What enables me to weather the storm that resulted from watching the woman I worship to the point of mild obsession suddenly remove my children from my life and cause half the people I love in my world to abandon me?

Allowing myself to feel what was expected of me was the right thing to do so nothing in terms of emotions was swept under the carpet. No denial or masking of the truth of what happened or how I was feeling ever took place. That's why I allowed myself to cry, to mourn, but that's where it stopped and I, myself, am proud of how I coped with the situation.

Through self-assessment, I learned that the safety net and emotional tools I use to assist myself through mourning the loss of my family inadvertently evolved from my triumph over years of chronic pain and the emotional hardship that accompanied it. These skills enabled me to wholly feel the reality of my new world, to go down momentarily but to get straight back up, focus and flourish as a new man.

My Back Story

I suffered horrific chronic pain for three years after spinal surgery in November 2014. Before the surgery, I was a successful competitive rower for Toowong Rowing Club in Saint Lucia, Brisbane. It was a common sight to see my gold medals proudly displayed on social media while embracing my mentors and dear friends of the club. I loved the sport. It's difficult to describe the sheer bliss of rowing through the fog during sunrise on glass-like water in perfect unison with my mates.

On one such morning, I recall being one hour into a hard session with eight men when everything around me fell into complete silence. Rowing at a high stroke rate, I fell into a dream-like state. My glare softened to a stare; my body sang on autopilot while I glided smoothly up and down the slides confidently, reefing the oar back to my lower ribs. I was sweating profusely but felt no effort whatsoever. I had goose bumps racing all over my body from head to toe in complete ecstasy. A massive amount of serotonin was being released in my brain from the finely tuned interaction with my comrades, the natural elements, water, air, and the fire in my quiet determination. The delicate dance with my trusted crew made me smile ear to ear as did the sound of soft tumbling bubbles under the hull, indicating that all things were working very, very well. I was addicted to it; my natural high, and the best kind!

This morning was shortly before my world fell apart. I didn't feel right in the lead-up to the annual Head of the Yarra, a big race involving clubs from all over the country, held in Melbourne, Australia. I had experienced mild back pain before, so I figured with some stretching and warming up, I'd be okay.

Only three weeks out from the interstate competition, I was in a great deal of pain during practice. I held on as long as I could. I'd pushed the grief aside for a few months already and assumed I could do it again. We'd trained tirelessly in a great crew perfecting the techniques for the event and I was one of the few big guys in the club working in the powerhouse (middle) of the boat. They needed me, but I couldn't survive any longer. I had to stop. Ashamed to let my team down, I dragged my oar blade on the water and yelled at the crew to stop. The men immediately decided to head back to the club to prevent further injury. I was shattered that I'd failed them.

This was the first time I felt the white-hot pain from the nerve damage. I moaned as we took the slow 20-minute trip back to shore, which felt like two hours. With one man down and a blade dragging on the water, it was a gradual return. I sat curled up on the slide, mind racing amidst the pain, assessing my body that I knew so well. I'd been playing competitive sports since I was five years old and was fully aware that I was in big trouble.

 We finally arrived back to shore and the men jumped out and took my blade. I hesitated, as one does with shooting pain, moving slightly in one direction, and then the other, feeling the strike repeatedly while attempting to navigate a way out of the long narrow boat. In the end, I had to crawl. I braced myself on hands and knees, panicking that the fire in my back would hit me again like a baseball bat striking deep in my core. James helped me to my feet as I gathered the courage to stagger up the ramp with a contorted abdomen that pushed my left shoulder in line with the center of my pelvis when I stood up. Unbeknownst to me, this default posture would return to twist me periodically for three years. As I shuffled towards the clubhouse, I heard Bob, our bowman, say, "Oh, that's not good." It wasn't. That was the last time (I thought) I would ever row with these wonderful men. The traumatic week that followed set up my next few years of pain and hardship.

Two times in the next week, I was rushed to the hospital from home. The ambulance officers knew I was a tough man—I told them so too—but they could see the state I was in and hurried to relieve me of my pain as the green morphine stick did nothing to stop it. They rushed the IV line into my arm to administer a dose of morphine to render me unconscious. Like something out of a movie, the blurred voices and white lights blended with various levels of pleasure, fear, and unconsciousness. That night in the hospital, I spent the entire time lying sideways with my legs hanging out of the bed near the floor. Even with strong pain relief, it was the only position that stopped the agonizing knives from digging into my back, sending lightning racing down my left leg. I later learned that my brain was contorting my body like a banana, separating the vertebrae to pull the protruded disc off the nerve. I was X-rayed and, to my surprise, that was all.

My private health insurance turned me down during this chaotic period, as my issue was deemed pre-existing; so, for a week, I was bounced around numerous public hospitals, none of which seemed to want anything to do with spinal injuries. I was given crutches in one hospital, a back brace in another, and a ton of drugs from all three. On your bikes, kids; good luck.

I woke up screaming on the living room floor one morning before going to see yet another specialist. Oh, the feeling of that whack deep in my core. My left leg was in a furnace. It was torture. In distress, and feeling helpless, my wife asked me what was happening as I started shaking all over. I told her I was going into shock through chattering teeth. I then pissed myself and passed out.

Finally, I was referred to a good surgeon in a private hospital and I put up the $15,000 for the operation. I couldn't carry on anymore in the state I was in, not to mention the pain. The surgery went well; I could feel that the immediate threat had been resolved, and to this day, I know they did the right thing in that theatre. My surgeon, however, showed me my amputated disc in a jar the morning after surgery. I don't know why he did that. With what I've now learned about pain concerning neuroscience and psychology, that was a very irresponsible thing to do. That vision with the neurological memory of the horrific pain would come back to haunt me. I went home on crutches the day after the operation with a bag full of opiate-based medication and confidence that 80% of the recipients who underwent my procedure would experience no further complications.

It became apparent very soon after that I was not one of that 80%. This was when things went sour for me again. I was not prepared for what was to come and how to deal with the plethora of physical and emotional complications that would plague me for three years.

System of a Down

Yes, the nerve was relieved, but the centers in my brain that were managing the pain continued firing rapidly. Why? Instead of improving, this problem got progressively worse over the coming years. I juggled various recovery methods for so long. Nothing seemed to work. The post-op X-Rays were fine, and that frustrated me as I needed to find the source of the pain. I fought with the idea that mental core exercises and Pilates would cure me. I tried it anyway, to no avail. The pain meds didn't help; they were band-aids that made me feel like a junky, and I was scared I would accidentally overdose. I told my doctor this in tears. Yet again, he sat quietly to write another script for Valium and Oxycontin, which I sometimes crushed and drank with whiskey to give the pain the middle finger, and to escape it for a few hours. I didn't need to do that. The meds were more effective when consumed normally, of course, but I was angry and self-sabotaging.

My pain ended up being like another entity within myself. I would speak to it, abuse it, and retaliate against it by consuming more alcohol and drugs. "Fuck you, you bastard. I'm in control tonight. See you tomorrow," I remember saying as I took another sweep of an Oxy infused Scotch single malt. This was a two-part solution: I'd escape pain as well as satisfy my brain's enormous thirst for endorphins that it once received from 12 hours of hard rowing per week. I felt I had lost myself and who I was. I was once a champion at anything I did, relied upon by my community as the strong man. Overnight all that was left was a near-crippled man at 31 years of age who couldn't even pick his infant son out of his cot or bend over to spit while brushing his teeth.

With the little time I had, and with the pressures of business and infant children, I also had to deal with the identity crisis and PTSD I was experiencing. After my surgery, I couldn't speak about it much. One night during a casual chat with a friend on the phone, he asked me about my situation. I had to cut the conversation short, and then I hid in the shower to cry uncontrollably for half an hour. I didn't know why that was happening. I was beyond depressed.

While still working every day to support my family and amidst periods of substance abuse to escape the intense pain, I sourced any information I could on the subject, as the doctors and specialists weren't helping. I also spent time researching chronic pain associated ADD as I was vexed as to why I couldn't concentrate. I would read half a five-line email, retain or understand none of it, and forget what I was doing. This led me to my first breakthrough!

The More You Think About It, The Bigger It Gets

Finally, something began to make sense. I learned that areas of my brain were being redirected and assigned an alternative function to focus on something else of seemingly greater importance—you guessed it, pain. But pain is not important in my case. I agree, but it doesn't matter. This functionality is called Neuroplasticity. It's the magnificent ability of the brain to change continuously throughout an individual's life. Until the 1970s, it was commonly assumed that the brain was hardwired after youth, but countless medical professionals have dispelled this. In more recent years, neuroplasticity knowledge has been made widely available to the public through incredible books like those from Norman Doidge, M.D. I became fascinated with neuroplasticity and even more so with what I learned immediately and over the coming years about the human ability to control it.

I was continually giving my pain so much attention that my malleable brain functionality devoted its workforce to it and, in turn, continued increasing and enhancing the neural networks associated with the problem! My point of focus caused my pain to grow and the capabilities that I normally excelled at, like reading and writing, were being severely affected. The vicious cycle repeated itself and intensified.

I was mismanaging the system that was in place to keep me safe by solidifying its existence with weak word and thought association. It was as simple as that. Bingo!

I learned that just like an avid guitarist may be brilliant with his excellent motor skills but still poor at soccer, or a great mathematician may be a below-average writer, the brain can recalibrate to support what it perceives as the most crucial of tasks. This function is what makes the hunter an epic shot with the bow because he practices that particular task all day. So, the evolutionary plastic brain delivers the skills it feels are required for that individual's lifestyle. It self-determines that the responsibility or activity regularly performed, spoken, or even thought about, must be of importance and crucial to his/her survival.

In my case, my brain's malleable feature devoted excessive resources to my ongoing and focused attention – my pain. Just like the ancient bowman, my mind was doing its job by strengthening neural pathways to enhance the effectiveness of the main focus of my attention. It was unaware, however, that it was doing me a great disservice. The brain does not know good or bad, pain or pleasure. It is a machine, acting under its environment and message inputs. Now that I was aware of this mechanism, how could I fix it?

I became very excited at this stage in my journey and so began my road to recovery.

Game Changer

I needed to change the way I think and talk about my pain, but how could I go from such a deep level of pain to no pain by simply thinking differently? Wasn't there something wrong in there beneath the skin in my back? My old belief system crept back in, but I pushed it away to apply a new model. In the coming days, I read more and began piecing together what I had already learned about the power of the mind. I had heard all the stories and techniques about manifestation and how to make your dreams come true. I never took to that modality. This new understanding was different, though. This was neurology and psychology, something that I had always been interested in learning more about over the years.

I remembered the studies about the placebo effect and stories about phantom limb pain (people experiencing pain in limbs that had been amputated) and the time I meditated my way out of anxiety at 22 years of age after hitting the wall from a year of consistent nightclubbing. Had I already known about, and practiced changing my mind? My emotions to a certain degree, sure; but pain? Was this possible?

I recollected Dr. Karl Kruszelnicki's story, which he told on ABC Radio some years ago. He was working in an emergency room at that stage of his career when, one evening, a motorcyclist was raced into the theater with broken bones and lacerations. While he was howling in pain, Dr. Karl placed an IV line into the patient's arm and advised him that he was giving him something. The patient assumed it was morphine and immediately enjoyed the relief of his injection. Much to Dr. Karl's surprise, the patient's heart rate dropped, his color came back to his cheeks, and he exclaimed that he felt better. However, the injection was only saline! Salty water!

Other staff members then administered morphine to the patient and he overdosed. Initially, his brain felt relief from what it thought was morphine and acted accordingly. Then when he received an actual morphine injection, his heart rate dropped too low as a result and they had to counter the potential overdose with another drug. Incredible! So I dived deeper into this world, understanding that there may be something there for me.

Results

After reading various books and applying what I already knew about the brain, I began implementing different techniques whenever I felt the pain coming or when I knew I was about to perform an action that would bring about pain. I needed to break the cycle I had created — the sequence I had previously reinforced via negative thoughts, words, and actions. I can attribute the first successes of my recovery to taking the time to understand the mechanics of the brain. It all started to make sense. The answers were there all along.

Owning the System:

Importantly, the first thing I did was to stop talking negatively about my body. I stopped using the word pain altogether. The signal coming from my lower back was only a sign and I knew that, actually, there was no issue in my back at all. It was all in my brain. I felt empowered already. I understood the mechanics of the system and I learned that, with a bit of effort, I could control it. If someone asked about my back while it felt like a busted old fishing rod, I'd say, "Yeah, thanks, it's pretty good." I am telling my brain it's good and it hears me. So perhaps the neural pathways might weaken and help me out here.

Distraction:

Moving forward, when I ran in a certain way that would generally bring about the pain, I would hum or squeeze my leg. This method was to distract my brain from focusing on the pain signals, a simple technique that provided results quickly. If I could keep from focusing on the issue, my pain was less intense. Think of this like throwing a biscuit to the angry dog to get his attention off you so that you can deliver the mail or how the high school bully, when you don't respond to his antics, loses interest and eventually does something else. These metaphors were handy for me in downgrading the issue and making the pain seem completely irrelevant. I was getting stronger. I was breaking free and, most importantly, feeling a reduction of discomfort (pain).

Movement:

When feeling restricted with spasms or pain, I would apply some of or all of the afore-mentioned techniques and keep moving. I don't recommend anybody exerting themselves beyond their capability. Still, for myself, I reaffirmed that I am safe to do that particular movement by slowly moving through it confidently but cautiously. With this, I was training my brain that the motions I wished to perform were safe and healthy, hence reducing the neural connections associated with the pain. The bully was getting bored.

Visualization:

This was probably the method that served me best. As I understood that pain was only signaling, whenever I felt pain, I visualized a roadblock in the middle of my back that wouldn't let any pain signals through it. They would approach looking like blue arrows in succession, hit the barrier, take a U-turn, and head back down. I would accompany this with an affirmation such as, "No. No, thanks. I'm busy, not today," and immediately shift my focus to something I was busy doing or something else of little to no importance.

Meditation:

Another robust method was actively using mediation to visualize the retraction of pain associated to neural pathways. I would picture my hijacked brain with octopus-like tentacles consuming it, which symbolized the centers dealing with pain. They were blue also for some reason. I would then visualize the tentacles retracting only to occupy a small blue dot. This was how I was considerably allocating my brain to deal with any pain in my body. After all, I still needed the mechanism within me to keep me safe. However, *I* was in control and provided it with what *I* thought was necessary to perform its duty. "I'm the boss; do what you're told."

I have meditated a lot over the years, and since my surgery, I studied and practiced it frequently once I learned its true effectiveness. It is evident to me that the application of my meditative techniques is 100% responsible for the full recovery of my emotional and physical self. After three years of suffering, I had no additional surgery nor used any new physical exercises. I felt relief from what I did with my mind. The byproduct of delving into meditation to save me from chronic pain is that, as a result, I drew all the emotional benefits from the practice, which has supported me to this day, particularly in dealing with the emotional hardship of my marital separation.

Clear Your Mind - No Thanks

There are many misconceptions relating to meditation. The first being that one must clear the mind to obtain inner peace; Nonsense! We must develop the ability to *handle* what happens in the mind to achieve peace rather than work on eliminating thoughts. For us Westerners, who absorb vast amounts of stimuli via countless input streams during our busy daily lives, the idea of clearing our minds for 30-60 minutes and thinking of nothing is ludicrous. If you are meditating as a beginner for inner peace or pain relief, focusing on the flame or the white light is only going to piss you off.

I teach people how to meditate during my Men's Retreats in Bali, Indonesia, and I constantly hear people say, "I can't meditate." Yes, you can. Everyone can; it's just that you've set unrealistic expectations for yourself, or you have the wrong idea about what meditation is. You're not a yogi in the mountains, and neither am I; acting like one or trying to achieve what they do is going to frustrate anyone.

Let me walk you through how I've done it for 15 years, the same way, and what it has provided me.

Meditation is weightlifting for the mind. For me, it is not a spiritual exercise at all. It is a neurological workout, a way to service and upgrade my internal computer system (brain). It is an effective way to raise my threshold for what I can handle, both emotionally and physically. I can say that meditation may have saved my life.

I sit, shut my eyes, breathe only through my nose and relax; pray to no one or nothing. Where my hands are comfortable, I let them rest, not concerned which fingers are elegantly touching each other or how I am going to look in the yoga class next week. Sometimes I think I must look like a hunched over, drunk and homeless guy, but I'm comfortable so I win.

Comfortably sitting, I let all things that need to arise come and go. I make them arrive without resistance while I observe them objectively. They go and I watch as I would if I were a patron in a movie cinema. I interpret thoughts if I want to and change them if I feel like doing so. I don't judge the stimulus or wonder why it's there. I let the brain throw around the multitude of visions, sounds, and the entire internal monologue it wants.

During the meditation practice, once I move through the irrelevant noise, my brainwave frequency drops.

This is where the magic happens. It's in this space that I gain clarity; everything automatically becomes quiet. Just like not giving the physical pain attention, the noise, fear, or whatever it is that's racing around in there will eventually dissipate. At this stage, a delightful physical sensation arrives in my body due to the endorphin release in my brain. That's right; all those feel-good chemicals. I can now choose when to release them to feel high! With full honesty, I can assure you that the highest I have ever achieved through various types of meditation — indescribable physical and emotional bliss—is possible without drugs. I can activate and enjoy these feelings whenever I want, and you can, too.

I feel I've regained a type of control of my neural networks and internal reactionary safety mechanisms by sitting quietly, with my mind proving to myself that I am not in danger. My thoughts are not me; they are just messages, interpretations of my internal hard drive (brain) that are harmless unless I decide they need to be addressed or utilized further. In conjunction with moving through emotional stress during meditation, one should also observe any physical pain as inconsequential, and stay with it for longer than you would typically move to be comfortable again. Over time, this increases your pain threshold and control over your automatic responses in daily life. You become emotionally and physically stronger.

This is the breakthrough: If I'm okay; better yet, comfortable with whatever happens in my mind and body, I can be comfortable with what happens in my daily life: I can survive physical pain.... my divorce!

The events that take place around us, the conversations (pleasant or otherwise), and the road traffic, are absorbed and processed by our minds in a conscious state. How does the brain's management of this stimuli differ from what happens in my mind while I am meditating? The fact is, it doesn't. It's the same, and the brain knows no difference. The same responses are triggered in varying degrees, whether we think about a tormenting situation, or we experience them in the physical sense. The triggers mean that, due to my commitment to meditation, I've created an ability to calmly process any event or stimulation from a place of composure, patience, and control, without fear.

I am no longer an Auto Response Mechanism delivering impulsive actions and responses. I've heightened my ability to move past my automatic stress responses. I can hold my breath for five minutes, sit cross-legged for ten days without speaking, swim the length of an Olympic-sized swimming pool underwater, walk on hot coals, row with my buddies again, go to the gym, and keep my chin held high through my recent separation.

That's right. It is medically proven that, with practice, people can regulate their body temperature, heal debilitating chronic pain and mood disorders, and boost the immune system with thought (meditation) alone. I am a living proof.

Imagine a world heavily populated with humans who can consciously choose how to respond to each other! Via a variety of forms of meditation, I have created a present space that is like a box, between the event and my response to the event, in which I now can decide which answer is best suited to that particular situation. I can slow down, breathe, and choose how to act, and at crucial times as well as to a greater degree, choose what and how to feel.

This system kept me in good stead through the waves of my divorce. The liberating space between the event and my response is the most powerful asset I own. I've cracked the code and mastered my mind. In contrast to my old behavioral patterns, I am today my own revised version of Strongman.

"Anyone can give up, that's the easiest thing in the world to do. But to hold it together when the whole world would understand if you fell apart, that's the real strength."

~ Unknown

CHAPTER FOUR

———— ❖ ————

Melanie's Garden

by Melanie Tan

"Y ou are so simple-minded, Mel," my life
coach friend said to me with such
disdain. While our conversation
continued, she rolled her eyes as I expressed inner
strength as a singular trait. She threw her arms up in
the air and said, "No, no, no! Mel!" Exasperated, she
explained that there are different types of inner
strengths: mental, physical, emotional, so on and so
forth. She went on to say that if you want to develop
REAL inner strength, try fasting for X amount of days.
She rolled her eyes at me again and stopped short,
trying to educate the simpleton before her.

Different types of inner strengths? And then, there's
REAL inner strength? What does not eating have to do
with building inner strength? Hmm... How my simple
mind finds it all so confusing. To be honest, before
having to write this, I never thought about inner
strength.

When asked if I wanted to be part of this project and
to write about developing inner strength, I knew

immediately that I did. Yes! The title completely resonated with me. I knew I could contribute. I had lots to share about this topic. I know that, over the years, I have done some things right to develop this thing, we call inner strength—even more so than others. I know it exists. I feel it. No, not that strong will or even mental strength that is so talked about these days. I'm talking about that innate strength that lies deep down in the depths of your being. The strength you didn't even know you had that is so abstract you can't even imagine its power.

As I started conversations about this topic, I discovered that, just like most intangible things, different people have different ideas about it or different ways of describing it. Some, like me, have never even thought about it. One thing for sure, it is a trait that can and needs to be developed for a fulfilling life. And it starts from the day we are born.

I like to think that life is like a garden. We are born with seeds to sow and nurture in the garden of life. One of those seeds is that of strength—not ordinary physical strongman strength, but the elusive dormant power from within. They say this type of force doesn't come from winning or from what you can do; this type of strength is developed through the struggles of life. And I've always felt like I was struggling since I was a little girl. I struggled within myself and definitely with others.

I'm not sure how or when this began for me, but the idea of not being good enough was embedded in my psyche.

Being the youngest of three children, I looked up to my siblings and thought for a long time that those who were older were wiser. I preferred to learn from these older folk. I was quite the copycat. I was very impressionable and always wanted to follow my siblings even when they didn't want me around. My mother tried to get me into reading, but I didn't take to it. I preferred exploring and using all of my senses. I learned to enjoy my own company and to play by myself. But life is to be shared, and it's always more fun with company.

It is said that the people in our lives are reflections of ourselves. The kind of relationships we have is dependent on our ability to foster these relationships, which in turn reflects our character. There is always something to learn from the people we meet. It is through my relationships that I've received the best life lessons, lessons that would help define me and become a source of inspiration and nourishment for my garden of life. As I transform, so do my relationships.

Relationships are the bane of my existence, but also at the core of my existence.

Family ties always get tested — the worst and longest for me being with my father. I remember being Daddy's girl. He would take me everywhere with him. I always used to insist that he kiss me goodnight before he went to bed. When I was about 11, I saw him being angry and violent with my sister and then with my mum. I tried to stop him, and he shouted loudly at me with his huge angry eyes. I became so afraid and sad. I felt betrayed. How could you treat someone like that when you are supposed to love them? That was the turning point of our relationship. In my teenage years, I became less sad and more rebellious. I held on to the anger for many, many years seeking solace in the company of those outside my home.

Friends are the flowers in the garden of life. They add so much color, beauty, and experience to life. Just as every flower fades, so do friendships. Then, new ones blossom. Bear in mind, also, that every rose has its thorns. Who needs enemies when you have friends? Friends will tell you what they think; they will bring you down, avoid you, talk behind your back, and hurt you.

I don't know why friendships have to be so complicated, but they are. There are expectations, judgments, and even jealousies.

When I was as young as eight years old, my best friend from school didn't like me hanging out with another friend. I didn't understand why I couldn't be friends with anyone and everyone. She stopped wanting to be best friends and we drifted apart. There's peer pressure. You must be like the others; otherwise, they don't want to be friends with you. When I was 14, I dated a girl. The group of friends I hung out with stopped talking to me. Just. Like. That.

From then on, I became a little jaded with the idea of friends and became more interested in my love life. I moved away from the group mentality and preferred a more intimate style of friendship. I led a nomadic lifestyle and moved around different circles. I met all sorts of people from different walks of life. I have been very fortunate to form incredible bonds even though they never lasted. In my life; friendships came and friendships went. It didn't matter then. That's just the way it happened; much like my love life.

I started dating at the age of 13 and never stopped. I was never short of suitors. When a relationship didn't work out, I never consciously looked for the next ones; they just came along. My heart got broken a million times into a million pieces. And even though I told myself many times not to give my heart away, I could never hold back.

When I was 17, I dated someone who was 24. I fell in love quickly and grew to love her very much. She was actually on the rebound and still in love with her ex when we got involved. She was a suicidal emotional wreck. We were staying in different countries when she overdosed, and I had to call her neighbor to save her. One time when we were together, she suffered a major asthma attack and stopped breathing as she lay in my arms on the way to the hospital. I didn't know what to do, but I knew I was not going to let her die. I shook and shook her and kept shouting her name. She eventually came to and made it to the hospital. She said that she felt so tired from all the drama with her ex and just wanted to leave it behind, so she stopped trying to breathe. It broke my heart to see her in so much pain.

I stayed on with the relationship and helped her get over her ex. She eventually cheated on me with a younger, sexier version of me. I was a tomboy who wasn't as sassy. Considering all that I had gone through with her, I was attached to her. However, it was a one-way street. This relationship—or the lessons from this relationship—stuck with me for a long time. She taught me about standards, and what it meant to project emotions on others; also that I was a pathological liar. She also used to call me a martyr— or, rather, tell me to stop being a martyr—which I didn't understand then.

One night, I was dancing by myself in a club, as I usually do, and this boy was dancing next to me. He didn't come and dance with me, like other boys. Week after week, he just danced next to me. He was different. He was exciting. We became friends and started to see a lot of each other.

So, at 19, I unexpectedly got involved with a boy. He was the first boy I ever became so very intimate with, and I wanted to be with him forever and ever. The problem is, there is no such thing as forever and ever. Well, except for change. Change is forever and ever.

The time came when I had to make a life-defining decision; I broke my lover's heart to be with him. I know I hurt her so badly, even though this had been one of the best relationships I have ever had. She was nothing but good to me. But it was fate. I felt I had to go. I knew then that I never wanted to hurt anyone like this again and made a resolve that this would be the last time. It was a difficult time, because I also had to deal with the backlash from friends. Who? What? When? How could I start dating a guy?

That decision marked the end of an era and the start of another that would shape the me today.

The next three years were a dizzying blur, living a life of decadence. The boy and I were very much alike; too much alike. We were total sensation seekers, addicted to the high life. We started to live in an illusion where life wasn't about each other anymore; it was all about heroin. Although we wanted to get married, it was impossible to make decisions or take action for the benefit of our future. We were stuck in the moment of constant craving. I didn't know what love meant anymore. It was the lowest point of my life having begged, borrowed, and stolen to feed the vicious cycle of soul destruction.

It was the time of my life that I rarely speak about to anyone.

Fortunately, my parents insisted I leave Australia and go back to Singapore. It was tough. I didn't want to leave the love of my life; but was that heroin or him? Ha! I was afraid, uncertain, and sick, both physically and mentally. I was completely lost as to what to do with my life. By this time, I was expected to go out into the workforce, and I was just not ready.

When I got back, I went in search of some heroin and got connected with an old friend. He turned out to be my savior, and put me on the road to recovery. It was no surprise that I became romantically involved with this friend. I entrusted him with my life, and I took the relationship very seriously. I hung on to his every word and followed all of his advice. I got a job, made money, and joined normal society. He led me down the path of sobriety and dignity, which did not serve him well.

As I started to gain some sense of myself, the relationship became difficult. Whatever I said, did, or wore was a problem. I was always doing something wrong. Little did I know he had emotionally abused and kidnapped me. After almost two years, we broke up. Or rather, I did something that made him very angry, and he just stopped responding to me. I tried and I tried to get a hold of him, but he stayed away from me like the plague. I was so guilt-ridden and miserable, blaming myself for being so stupid. Why did I make such a foolish decision that cost me the best thing in my life? Why?

A little over a month of beating myself up, a woman approached me at work. She introduced herself, and then asked me if I was Melanie Tan and if I was dating this man. I said that I was not anymore. Something clicked in my head and I asked her if she was dating him. She said that she had been, and it would be one year next month. Oh my! We had a good chat and decided to confront him. She was working with him that night in a private environment, and so we went ahead with our plan. He proved himself an egomaniac, never admitting he had been cheating on either of us.

I decided it was time to move on. A friend introduced me to someone, and we hit it off. When the narcissistic ex-boyfriend saw us together, he started to stalk me, playing emotional games, asking me if my new lover knew about my past. He would say, "No one will love you the way I do. No one will take care of you like I did." Although I never went back to him, the insecurities about me, lingered within.

One of the worst endings to a love affair is an unexpected turn of events that forces the relationship to end when neither wants it to. I got into a whirlwind romance once with a guest at the hotel where I was working. It was love at first sight! He came to the concierge counter to talk with the bellman. As he was talking, I looked up from my work and at the same time, he turned to look at me. Our eyes caught each other and there was this—what do you call it?— current, electricity, buzz, an unmistakable attraction. He was older, sophisticated and charming. We only dated for a short time when he left and never returned. I became so despondent. I later found out he went to prison in China for ten years.

The guy I dated afterward also ended up in jail. But I was much more vested in that relationship. We'd been dating for almost two years. Up till then, that was the most devastating moment of my life. Although I knew the moment would come when he would have to go, I was not emotionally mature enough to handle the situation. When his sentence of ten years was announced, I broke down. Life after that was miserable. I could not eat. I didn't feel like going out. I stopped going to work. I only slept and smoked cigarettes for weeks. I was an emotional wreck, always thinking about the cruelty of life. The whys were never-ending.

I've been told that what I experienced was depression.

It was this adversity that brought the focus back to friendships. I needed help. It was interesting to see how people reacted to this incident. Some left, some stayed, some tried to take advantage, and some angels appeared. This incident made me value the people in my life who helped in some small or big way. I started to put more effort into maintaining the friendships that I had.

After the incident, I decided to go to the UK. I went on a working holiday visa and spent two years there. I went to be with someone, actually, but he broke up with me about a month before I was to leave. I was heartbroken, but I'd always had my reservations about him. He was much younger than me, and was just starting university in a new country. And I know what that is like! By that time, I had the attitude that if you love someone, you should let them go. And if it was meant to be, they will come back. Therefore,, I decided to go anyway. I landed at Heathrow Airport on a cold January morning with my life in my suitcase. I sat on it, lit a cigarette and wondered, what am I going to do? I had £2000 in my pocket, no friends, and nowhere to stay.

By now, I knew myself to be a survivor.

It was the first time in a long time that I was by myself, with myself. It was the longest time I had ever been single—almost one year. Being away from Singapore in a different environment, I tried to be more open. With no lover to distract, I spent my energy on developing the beautiful friendships I made.

It was inevitable that I would meet someone. He was funny and we shared the same ideals and aspirations. He was totally in love with me, and he was very passionate and expressive. I, not so. He found it very difficult to manage me, and I found it very difficult to articulate my feelings. This is not the first time a partner had made me aware of this. The relationship didn't work out and we broke up.

Many of my experiences in the UK were a repeat of the past. It was a humbling epiphany that I had been going round in circles. I'd had enough of my own nonsense. I realized that I don't want to just survive; I want to thrive. It was time to make different choices so that I could get different results. I decided that I would do things differently. I would start choosing the opposite of what I would typically choose.

When I returned to Singapore, I dated someone I never thought I would. He was that typical white ex-pat guy who was the lady's man. He was about 12 years older than me. I approached the relationship differently. I was more vocal, more persistent, and more confident. I grew to like him, but I knew he was dating other people, so I also chose not to commit myself. We only dated for a short time. But it was so significant, because he helped me to realize that I had come far from the naive little girl I had been, and helped me to break free from my belief that older people are wiser.

At the same time, I was spending a lot of time with a boy whom I knew from years earlier. He was an unlikely prospect, but in the spirit of doing things differently, I let one thing lead to another. I fell completely in love with him. He turned out to be the rock-solid foundation that I needed. There was a simplicity about him that captured my heart, and a sincerity that nourished my soul. We wanted to help each other grow. It's been 13 years now and counting.

Now that my love life has started blossoming on solid ground, all of my other relationships began to wilt and wither away.

One of the most significant of these losses was the most heartbreaking and life-changing time of my life; it was when a childhood friend took his own life. He was my best friend in the neighborhood. We grew up together and shared our teenage angst. He was a brother to me. We lost touch in our late teens when I moved to Australia and he moved to Japan.

I was 29 when I returned from the UK and we reconnected. By then, he was married, and was facing some marital problems. He came to see me with his problems and told me his thoughts of suicide and even of having tried to do it. Out of all the possible options, why choose the one that stops giving you options? I remember asking him that. I did what I could to dissuade him from taking such action. Things seemed to get better for him after a while and he stopped talking about suicide.

Then, I went away for work. When I returned to Singapore, I tried calling him, but I couldn't get through. After a couple of weeks of not being able to get in touch with him, I called his wife. She broke the news to me. I was in disbelief, confused, speechless, and I became very sad. The pain ate into my heart as I tried to move on with life as if nothing had ever happened. People come in and out of my life all the time; I should be used to it by now. But this was the first time I had faced the death of someone I had been so close to.

I felt like I lost everything.

This loss created the most significant degree of grief I had ever experienced. But I did not realize it at the time. The effects were unprecedented. I channeled the grief by becoming obsessed with friends and concerned for their happiness, which mutated me into being overbearing and insecure. It was the start of a storm that would threaten to destroy the seedling of inner strength that I had been unconsciously cultivating.

More losses were to come.

Relations with a close friend became very strained. I had met her when I returned from the UK and we got along like wildfire. I grew to be very fond of her and looked up to her. She was the corporate high flyer I thought I wanted to be. And we became very close. But all that changed when I started wakeboarding. I realized that I didn't want to be that kind of woman. I began to discover my essence. And that led to a lot of friction and drama between us. The friendship as we knew it came to a tragic end.

Around the same time, my best friend of 20 years said to me that she didn't want to be that kind of friend anymore, meaning she didn't want to be best friends anymore. I hadn't seen it coming. Of course, she had her reasons—I was needy, self-righteous, and had said things she didn't like. I was crushed and confused. I let her say her piece and left it at that. There is nothing you can do when someone doesn't want to be with you. Breakups are hard.

In the five years that followed my friend's suicide, I was to face the death of a loved one at least once a year, including my grandmother and my sister's best friend. Two friends whom I was getting close to also took their own lives. I'd canceled a meeting with one of them only a few days before he died. The agony, guilt, and sorrow were too much. The pain could not be ignored anymore. What was going on with me?

Everything was falling apart. I was falling apart. Someone said to me that I care too much about my friends. I should leave them be and focus on myself.

By this time, Vipassana meditation had come into my life. I went for my first course in 2009. I went only to find out what it was about and thought I would never go back. In 2012, I noticed an email for a three-day course. They were looking for volunteers to serve for the course. For some reason, the idea to serve appealed very much to me and, since it was only three days, I thought I could manage. It was the beginning of a brand-new journey.

I learned about the organization; how they operated and the help that they needed to run a course. I learned that, although I had been through a course, I had no idea what Vipassana meditation was about at the time. Moreover, there was so much more to learn. I became genuinely interested in the practice and helping the organization. I continued to volunteer for the rest of the year, and I committed myself the following year, to volunteer and learn more about Vipassana.

The process brought me back to my own heart. I had forgotten the most important relationship: the relationship with my self—with the mind, body, and spirit. I was completely disconnected. I have never taken care of myself. I have put myself through a lot of pain. I've carried the burden of the consequences of my actions all these years, wondering how to make things right. I have always thought of my life as one big mess, and I have even been told that it was. My confidence was merely a facade as I allowed guilt and shame to reside in my heart. As a teenager, I had promised myself that I would live life without regrets, and that had definitely helped me to get so far. But to go further and continue living without worry and despair, I needed to accept and own up to the path I had taken. I needed to let go of all the misery I had accumulated and held onto in life.

Vipassana meditation became the cathartic release I needed and the nourishment for the seeds in my garden.

I found that the first step to nurturing the seed of inner strength is forgiveness; not the forgiveness of others, but of ourselves. Forgiveness is the key to personal empowerment. We live so harshly, always criticizing and blaming ourselves, which we then project onto others. I came to realize that there is no such thing as a mistake. Everything serves a purpose. We are here to learn what it means to be human—to experience, master life, and evolve.

Inner strength is not tied to mental ability, but rather the capacity of the heart.

It is not about being strong-willed, harsh, or strong in the physical sense. It is about being kind, patient, and compassionate. This is the type of strength that dwells within your soul's purpose. That is why the idea of inner strength seems intense and elusive, because it's tied to the purpose of our human life. As long as we haven't figured it out, life will keep flowing with its lessons to teach us how to cultivate that exceptional seed.

It is said that we have all the answers; we just need to settle our minds so that they can arise from deep within us. The technique of Vipassana has taught me how to settle my mind. Learning how to observe my entire being—mind and body—has given me amazing insights. And this has helped me to make sense of it all.

Inner strength is nourished by trust, peace, and love. These are the richest nutrients you can give your seed. Strength, to me, is the freedom that gives us the ability to do what we need and want. Doubt, fear, and anxiety will always be there, but these things have no hold on you. In my pure mind, inner strength is the bedrock and source for all other character traits that are needed for a fulfilling life. Fasting for however long will be a breeze. The physical, mental, and emotional states will be stable and balanced in times of any kind of distress.

We just need to remember that in every adversity lies the seed of an equal or greater opportunity. Have the trust. Be at peace. Feel the love.

"Strength does not come from physical capacity it comes from an indomitable will."

~ Mahatma Gandhi

CHAPTER FIVE

❖

Intuition – Your Inner Strength, Your Super Power

By George Kaponay

"The seemingly unanswerable questions should be embraced and not rejected. Mystery and the mysterious should be allowed a space to thrive and enthrall us."

~Kingsley L Dennis - *Healing the Wounded Mind*

What if I were to start by saying that, in finding your true inner strength in this life, you might have to consider that you are something—someone far more significant than you have ever thought possible? What would you feel? What if what you are is more akin to the power of infinite suns than a dull, expendable, light bulb?

Does this thought consciously challenge you?

What if the obstacles that keep you from realizing such inner strength are a result of the   choices you have made, the unnecessary burdens you have carried, the positions you have been goaded into choosing, and the subsequent roles you have settled on and locked yourself into? What if I were to share with you that through a simple process of letting go, resetting the framework of how you see the world, venturing into the unknown with confidence, and asking questions of a limitless nature, you could access a reliable Super Power to serve you when needed on your journey of life. Furthermore, you would realize the Super Hero you really are.

Is this all too much to consider? If not, then, with loving kindness, I invite you to read on.

When I delivered a talk at the Home Schoolers' Conference of California in San Jose recently, an attendee approached me. Something I'd said had resonated with her concerning issues with the choices she'd been making in her life.

What I said was, "The concept of *comfort* and the accompanying societal narrative that we should strive for a *comfortable life*, was to the human psyche, the equivalent of cancer." It is that stagnation of development that psychologically and energetically boxes us into apredetermined glass ceiling set of outcomes in our minds; one that shuts us off from the ever-changing dynamic nature of this existence, and our ability to affect it through our own self-determination.

The Choices We Make
And How We Define Them

How often do you hear this expression: *I just want to be comfortable!*

During the course of traveling the world with my family for the past nine years, I am convinced that had we not chosen the challenging and, perhaps at times, uncomfortable situations we faced, our personal development, the intrinsic nature of our awareness, and the meaning we have drawn from these experiences, would have been compromised. We would have been undermining the core of our integrity and authenticity, ignoring fundamental waypoints to finding our true worth.

But how do we stand firm in integrity while facing what appear to be some of the toughest decisions we have to make in life? Consider that in choosing the least obvious—sometimes the outwardly perceived harder choices— perhaps we are actually raising our stakes and thereby multiplying exponentially the potential of receiving a far higher dividend and return on investment from this experience of life.

Perhaps, also, the hard choices we face need not be viewed or understood to be *hard choices*. Instead, with a slight resetting of the framework of our minds, calibrated to meet the dynamic nature of our universe, we could embrace the challenges we face as the necessary capital investment, even the catalyst to realizing the inner strengths we possess.

Resetting the framework of our minds, removing and releasing the burden of weight of what is hard, opens us to limitless potential outcomes. As opposed to squandering the power of our thoughts on lamenting how *hard* things are, we can instead make a conscious leap to seeing an event as an opportunity for development, no matter what packaging it is delivered in. The way we choose to see and accept things correlates to the ease with which we can navigate this reality.

Awareness Of Our Accepted Realities

But what are the determining factors in our lives that make us see things in the ways that we do? How did you come to accept who you are? By the time we reach adulthood, there are a bastion of belief systems that we have been taught or have adopted as immutable. Thus, through this willing acceptance, we limit our understanding of who we are, and downgrade the trajectory of what we can choose and who we can become.

But how does one become aware of potential limiting beliefs holding him back from seeing the limitless potential of his life? This is where that Superpower comes into effect. YES, you are a Superhero, and YES, you have a Superpower, the Superpower of *Intuition*.

This is that inner voice of guidance that most people in the world are well practiced at ignoring.

Our Superpower

Whether you have heard its calling, and whether you've utilized it or not, it is important to know that this Superpower, engaged, will enable you to push the envelope of your life and reality to where you will never feel the harsh pull of its gravity. Intuition is an inherent human tool that allows you to anticipate the curves and bends of this existence, so that you can lean into the turns and get the most out of the ride without the fear of falling. Intuition acts as a type of directional guidance, opening us to the awareness of possibilities and potentials to live a fuller and richer experience of life's choices without fear. It helps us to reset limiting frameworks, where previously challenging decisions now become the natural choices you have always known you needed to take. It allows us to acknowledge the Superheroes we are.

Over the last 12 years, as a family, we have made it a conscious imperative to listen intently to this call of intuition and to trust its direction and guidance in our journey of traveling and learning.

Our Journey Of Realization

Prior to realising we had this Superpower, we too were that mild-mannered family, living in Metropolis, encapsulated and paralysed by our own fears, uncertainties, and pressures that we, ourselves, society and loved ones were heaping upon us. It was around 2008 when both my wife and I started to feel that our lives were no longer our own, that we were no longer the captains of our journey. I was working at an unsustainable 80 hours a week in the software industry as a professional sales manager, reaching the verge of burnout. We were spending less and less time together as a family. Our children were enrolled in school and almost every kind of extra-curricular activity. As early as the first grade, we started to see disturbing things from their experiences in school. One afternoon, our daughter, Réka, came home telling us that one of the other girls had been telling her not to play with Sindhu because she had dark skin. My wife, Bobi, and I were gobsmacked.

Despite feeling a deep despair in her heart, Bobi decided to invest her energies to research all sorts of alternative ways we could be together as a family. This slight resetting of the framework of her outlook was the differentiating factor.

While she discovered that there was a thing called homeschooling, it was where she dug deeper at more intrinsic and inviting questions that she found direction. Questions concerning our role as the parents of our children and what we envisioned this to be took centre stage. While we took such great care to bring these children into the world and held the best of intentions for their education, it became clear that we were surrogating our responsibility to raise them to others. Also, we were missing out on the massive gift of being with them and experiencing the opportunity to learn and grow together.

These questions and our realizations drew quite a stark and yet startling awareness within us, as if we had both just awoken from a long sleep. We were realizing that we were living lives that weren't of our own design. Yes, we had chosen them, but it became evident that we had made these choices based on specious premises and assumptions that we ourselves, through our own schooling, society, and family, were taught and accepted to be true.

These questions didn't go away. Now that we had opened the door, the necessary types of books and themes came to us as if by magic. It was not magic in the Harry Potter sense; it was our willingness to give more volume to that inner voice, and this Superpower was now willing into being the new things we needed to be open to discovering.

We discovered and read books like *Anastasia: The Ringing Cedars of Russia* by Vladimir Megre, The *Biology of Belief*, by Bruce Lipton, *The Divine Matrix* and *Fractal Time*, by Gregg Braden, and *A Course in Miracles*, opening ourselves to the possibility that the concepts in these books might challenge the very core and every precept our current realities were based on. It was this willingness to let go and venture into what for us was the relatively unknown, which empowered our intuition to guide us to take and learn what was relevant, to leave what was not, and to attune ourselves to opportunities that expanded our awareness for what was possible for us at that moment. It gave us the confidence to intentionally listen to and carefully act on that inner voice. This voice continually grew louder as we went along.

We started discussing about what this *new life* would look like, over the weekends and the evenings we were able to spend together. We asked the question - *How could we do this together?*

Even after looking at it from varying perspectives, there seemed to be great obstacles. *How would we earn money? How would we manage our time? How could we undo the damage done?* However, in practicing listening to our intuition, we were asking these questions in a different manner. We were asking them with a sense of the limitless in mind, and by asking questions that were challenging our status quo of comfort and seeing it for the debilitating condition it was, we were now upping the stakes exponentially, while also actively shedding our previously accepted mild-mannered existence in Metropolis. With this slightly shifted framework of mindset, guided by this Superpower, we were seeing a matrix of experiences that dynamically and consistently adapted their recognizable forms to us through our detailed conscious thoughts, rising up to meet us precisely at the point where we were ready to act. This is the essence of intuition. It is listening to and taking the lead from that Superpower that connects us to every aspect of this existence.

And, as it happened, on one Australian winter's morning in 2008, stuck in rush hour traffic and pouring rain, Bobi had never felt that call of intuition more strongly. It was a guiding light that allowed her to finally ask herself, *why are we continuing to do this?* At that moment, she knew that we no longer needed to keep subjecting our children and our family to this artificially created stress that was continually seeping into every aspect of our lives and, in the process, alienating us from each other. We could change everything by just letting go. It was at that very point of determination where intuition finally met resolution. In that one moment, we were committed to acting on that inner guiding voice. In choosing that specific intention to change, all the directions to all questions we were previously stuck on came naturally.

Within three weeks of deciding to home school, my work position was made redundant, assisted by an atypical tech giant firm and their reactionary decision to arbitrarily reduce seven percent of its workforce. With this decent payout, we were gifted the out we were looking for. We sold our house; or rather, got rid of our mortgage. We sold, gifted, or donated most of everything we owned, things that we hadn't used in years and were cluttering up our home our garage, our minds, and our lives.

Over a year's time, our continuous questioning and innate desire to live in freedom from limitations and expectations of others, gave us the confidence to consciously choose family as a priority over all other things. We had no idea what our income source would be, but the uncertainty of this did not stop us from venturing into the unknown and exploring different possibilities. We took our children out of a traditional school setting. We empowered them to learn freely from what inspired them in the moment. In doing so, we all learned together from what inspired each of us. This allowed us to encourage our children to also become our mentors and teachers, as well as enabling them to be full stakeholders in the decision-making process in our family, all when they were just eight years old. We created a consciously energized space of love where our collective sense of curiosity and our search for more clarity and adventure became our future. We deliberately chose meaningful work, the types of work that we created from following our intuitions, work that would keep us together. Through our first confident steps, we were starting to feel our conscious choices becoming fluid and natural in a way that they had never been before, as if we were willing them into existence. We embraced the inner Superheroes that we are and welcomed them to confidently guide us in our choices in life.

Following our intuition—letting go of the perceived security and comfort we were clinging onto so tightly—was the one choice that we needed to take so that we could change the trajectory of our lives. That decision subsequently allowed us to travel, to live and learn from the cultures, people, and places of over 50 countries on six continents. More than this, the experiences we've lived through have developed in us a sincere gratitude for all of life and living. It has allowed us to embrace any situation with the power of our choices, particularly when it meant going completely against the grain of what society or our family and friends were advocating for us.

It also led us to create *The Intuition Game*, a game designed intentionally for people and families to be able to access their Superpowers in a fun way together. *The Intuition Game* allows you to ask the most relevant questions concerning the direction of your life. We made this into a game partially because of our children, but also because, during the course of game playing, we can actually challenge ourselves to explore and question the deepest aspects of who we are as human beings, without it being too threatening. Accessing intuition in a game setting can also help us to break down daily barriers, and relieve ourselves of the roles we play and the perceived divides between us. This will help us to see more clearly the things that connect us rather than the things that divide us. *The Intuition Game* can do more than give you all a sense of shared direction; it can deepen your connection in a way that opens up new possibilities for you all to be the Superheroes of your own family story.

Ridding Ourselves Of Unnecessary Burdens Resetting A Framework Of Mind

Am I advocating that you sell everything and travel the world to find your inner strength, to hear your intuition and develop your inner Superpower? Well, perhaps in a metaphoric way, I am. Acknowledging the need for release and the catharsis that comes with this is a transformative step on the path to tuning into your intuition. The willingness to let go, to release the things and situations that no longer serve you, to relieve yourself of the unnecessary burdens that you carry, is a major step towards the confidence of knowing that something better, something more meaningful and fulfilling, is waiting for you. Adapting this mindset is a complete reset of the fear-based, lacking mentality that is such a prevalent foundational precept of our society. In a world where hoarding is elevated as the pinnacle of success, and where accumulation permeates every aspect of our consciousness and behaviors (even our relationships and work), I can appreciate just how much letting go without knowing what is coming may sound challenging.

Too often, most people only choose to let go in order to receive something new when they face harsh, unexpected challenges, such as when confronted with a life-threatening illness, a relationship ending, losing a livelihood, or some other traumatic situation. Even in our entertainment, the stories we are sold imply that catharsis can only happen when our heroes and heroines hit rock bottom, lose everything, or experience some harrowing event before a light bulb of revelation appears to them. It comes down to believing that you have to accept the painful experience of these seeming dead ends before the reward is available to you. This is why people avoid change like it is the plague, because it is consistently associated with the need to wallow in pain first. No pain, no gain, right? This is also why so many people will spend years consciously choosing to ignore the most prominent road signs from their intuition to embrace change and let go of things in their lives that no longer serve them.

As a family, we have walked the entire Camino de Santiago - the Norte route in 2015 and the Frances route in 2018. The Camino itself is an 800 km walk through the north of Spain. Let me say that when you walk 800 km / 500 Miles (most days walking 25-30 km

/ 15-19 miles), you are hyper-aware of even those extra few sips of water that you are carrying in your water bottle, strapped to your backpack. You are ready to strip everything away from your back just so that you can make the daily walk that little bit more bearable. You become mindful of the lightness in every single step you take and give thanks and acquire a new and deeper appreciation for a world that is unburdened of unnecessary weight. So why do we continually insist on accumulating more baggage every day?

Taking First Steps With Confidence

How can we develop this verve for change in a way that it is natural, uplifting, and dare I say intuitive, so that it invites ease and joy into our existence and reminds us of the Superheroes we are?

One of the easiest ways is to throw out the tangible things that no longer serve us. I mean, where possible, pass on things you no longer need to others who are in need. Do this mindfully. Go out of your way to find those who can make meaningful use of your things. This, too, will bring new connections, potentially new possibilities, into existence. With the things that do not find a distinct home, sell them, pass them on to Goodwill or other charities, recycle them, or even take them to the dump. You will be surprised just how much lighter you will feel physically and how your energy will increase.

Ask Questions With The Limitless In Mind

The slightly more demanding steps are to ask questions that challenge your status quo of comfort. Questions like, *What are the situations/work engagements/relationships that I am invested in that are no longer in alignment with my well-being, and what am I not seeing about them? What do I need to see here that I am not seeing presently? What is the change that I need to invite into my life now? How can I attract the best possible outcome in my life? What else is possible here that I could not even imagine?*

Start making affirmations that invite the limitless into your daily being without the affliction of fear. Say, for example: *I invite the necessary change into my life that will remind me of who I am and what I am capable of.* Investing time and effort to mindfully contemplate each of these parts of your life will put you in touch with that intuitive feeling about each of these areas. You will know unequivocally where you feel physical dis-ease, and this is your carbon monoxide detector showing you what you need to let go of. There is a reason why people refer to intuition as a gut-feeling: because it speaks to you via that physical feeling in your stomach. When something is off, you feel that dis-ease, whereas when you receive that warm and welcoming feeling, you know it is the way to go.

Asking these more in-depth, challenging questions, opening yourself to them from a limitless mindset, allows for mindful reflection and fearless contemplation. This simultaneous tuning into our energies and merging the mind with the physical feelings guided by our intuition, enables us to change a mindset, and in such a mind space, letting go ceases to feel painful; it is no longer associated with loss, and this empowers us with a sense of liberation. This is the liberating act of resetting that framework and the first step to accepting and trusting in our intuitions—our directional compasses— our Superpowers— which clears the way for us to accept ourselves as the real Superheroes we already are.

Shedding Our Belief In The Onscreen Superhero For The Ones We Already Have

It can be so easy to doubt our Superhero nature when we have come to believe that we need Superheroes to save us. The swathe of Superhero movies we have been swamped with over the past ten years only confirms how much it has been hammered into our psyches that we are mere mortals, desperately in need of saving, and incapable of saving ourselves. Why do we even need saving? People have lost themselves in a self-created maze, in a narrative waiting for a savior to come.

Our societal structures have also misled and manipulated us into taking stances and sides on intentionally misleading issues, as if our participation was mandatorily woven into the very fabric of our

DNA. They encourage us to own and defend issues that are *counterintuitive* to who we are. The false investitures society encourages us to bestow on ourselves and our children, have convinced people that they are a Democrat or a Republican, a proud meat-eater or a defensive vegan, rich or poor. They beg us to adopt a position and defend it with all of our might to the death. In this process, we adopt someone else's view of the world, someone else's feelings, someone else's emotions, someone else's outrage, and detrimentally, someone else's truth and measure of what is meaningful, fulfilling and purposeful to invest our lives in. And in playing their game, we lose our own integrity and forget about the guiding Superpower and the Superheroes we are.

In this situation, it stands to reason that we must contemplate and resolve the enigma of the very nature of our being. This reminds me of an allegory by Anthony De Mello, a Jesuit Priest, considered by many to be a pioneer of awareness and the practice of mindfulness.

A man found an eagle's egg and put it in a nest of a barnyard hen. The eaglet hatched with the brood of chicks and grew up with them.

All his life, the eagle did what the barnyard chicks did, thinking he was a barnyard chicken. He scratched the earth for worms and insects. He clucked and cackled.

And he would thrash his wings and fly a few feet into the air.

Years passed and the eagle grew very old. One day he saw a magnificent bird above him in the cloudless sky. It glided in graceful majesty among the powerful wind currents, with scarcely a beat of its strong golden wings.

The old eagle looked up in awe. "Who's that?" he asked.

"That's the eagle, the king of the birds," said his neighbor. "He belongs to the sky. We belong to the earth—we're chickens." So the eagle lived and died a chicken, for that's what he thought he was.

So How Can You Find Your Way Out Of This Chicken Coup?

At the beginning of this chapter I asked you to contemplate that, in finding your true inner strength in this life, you might have to consider that you are something—someone far more significant than you have ever thought possible, something more akin to the power of infinite suns than a dull, expendable, light bulb. I trust that, in reaching the end of this chapter, you can start to see—or rather feel—whether this is true for you. Just for a moment, contemplate how stark a contrast a Superhero and a chicken are to our psyches. Consider that, in living like chickens, we produce fantastical alternate realities and insane narratives throughout our existence just so that our self-curated fantasy world of pain and suffering doesn't split at the seams. By insisting on continuing to believe that we are indeed weak, mortal, and perishable, we do great damage to our self-perception, which results in the creation of all of the modern ills we experience in this world. Practicing letting go, resetting the framework of how you see the world, venturing into the unknown with confidence in whatever it is your heart calls you to, and asking questions of a limitless nature opens up the possibility for us to lean into and trust our intuition. Consulting it and acting on its directions can save us from ourselves.

And it is by the conscious choices we make every moment of every day; the carefully chosen words we speak—the authentic actions we take from the direction our intuition can provide—we come to realize our true inner strength, and then we can become the Superheroes we always have been.

"Your inner strength is your outer foundation."

~ Allan Rufus

CHAPTER SIX

❖

The Reality of Resilience is Time

By Richard Ayling

I woke up, clutching my stomach in agony. I rushed to the bathroom.

To my horror, I noticed that I was passing blood on the toilet.

The shock of that fateful morning, and visiting the hospital, with all the tests and the waiting, was the culmination of the life style choices I had been making. *What you do has a consequence,* I finally realized. I was told by the doctors that - out of the blue - I had inflammatory bowel disease, and that it would be with me for the rest of my life. At the ripe old age of 26, I had been given the biggest wake-up call you can imagine.

And you know what?

It was the best thing that ever happened to me.

Not at first, of course. But let me backtrack a little to set the scene.

It's 2006. I manage a bar-restaurant full-time in the UK, working shifts late into the night. It's one of the busiest in town. I start early in the morning, setting up the bar and doing the accounts, placing orders and drinking a lot of coffee. When the bar opens, I'm back helping out the other members of staff during the busy lunch period, ferrying around food and taking orders. At 2 pm, I get a three-hour break, little time to do anything significant after I've arrived home and done some basics. Then it's back to work. We get a lot of people in for dinner - the food is great, and at night the place is often packed, especially at weekends. To make the evenings more fun, I have a little drink behind the bar. Once we close up and finish cleaning, it's late, but one more drink (or two) won't hurt. Then to bed, or if it's the weekend, out to a club, partying until the early hours.

This is my life. Rinse and repeat. I've been doing this for two years.

My body will soon say something about this lifestyle, but right now, I'm caught in a loop.

And behind the lifestyle, something much more problematic: a mindset has slowly been forming, and it's not a positive one.

Before this job, I was working as a salesman, selling hi-fi and home cinema equipment. Earning money to make ends meet, simply. Neither position was inspiring nor what I wanted to do. The trouble was that I didn't know what I wanted to do other than write music and Dj. Just a few years before, I was at my happiest playing bass guitar in a band and producing electronic music. I felt alive and creative. I dedicated a lot of time and even focused my university education on music. After that, I wanted to expand my horizons and live in a bigger city. But after relocating, I struggled to find anyone to work with and began to feel isolated. Collaboration is a beautiful thing, although it does present challenges.

The writing was slow. What I had written, I wouldn't play to anyone. I DJ-ed here and there, but not all that much. I wasn't putting myself out there, instead I was holding back and staying in the comfort zone of my own creation. Retrospectively, I can now easily see that out of the fear of failure, and the fear of not being good enough at my passion, I'd somehow managed to convince myself that the path of creativity was an indulgence and not something I could make money with or spend any real time on. So, it became a hobby and a source of frustration. What a sadness that is. I'm now of a very different mindset and enjoy creating music for the sake of it, but back then, I was simply blocked. I can remember looking at other musicians and feeling very critical and envious. I became cynical. Moreover, I was now 'stuck' in a bar job that had minimal prospects for growth. And the final tonic…my relationship was in a very unhealthy place too.

This was a tough place to be in, and to avoid dealing with the unpleasant feelings I was experiencing, I numbed myself by eating and drinking to excess. I stopped taking care of my body and gained a reasonably impressive beer belly for someone who was so naturally lean.This then led to self-judgment and shame…perhaps you can see where this is going. Anger and frustration built up (sorry everyone back then), and as I rejected my life and my stomach, they started to reject me. I received some spectacular warning signs in the form of 'malodorous gases' (as doctors politely refer to them!), with friends and coworkers in the bar begging that I get myself checked out. I did a foolish thing and ignored these signs, and I paid the price.

Almost-rhetorical note to reader: If this happens to you, get yourself checked out. Now. Don't do what I did. When your body speaks to you (yes, even like this), pay attention and listen to it.

When I look back, I realise I actually spent over four years with this mindset and lifestyle. During this time, I moved from anxiety to depression and back again, the full spectrum. I was unfulfilled, going nowhere and knew it, but felt stuck and afraid to do anything about it.Then one morning, I woke up in agony, and everything changed.

I was diagnosed with Ulcerative Colitis, an autoimmune disease that inflames the colon, a condition also known as IBD. There was little information around at the time, and the roots of colitis remain a mystery even today. What is known is that for some reason, the immune system becomes so inflamed that it starts attacking itself, which is why the lining of my colon broke down and I suffered so much pain. I would go on to spend many more hours in the bathroom in misery. The doctor prescribed cortisone, which did reduce the inflammation, but as a side effect I suffered weeks of insomnia.

I'm grateful for the doctors as they did the very best they could for me, but receiving the diagnosis of a lifelong illness, seemingly out of nowhere, was hard and a sense of powerlessness prevailed. *Why me? Why now? What does this mean?*

It's normal to feel sorry for ourselves in these moments. It's a natural and healthy release. I was grieving what I believed to be a loss - of the kind of life that I used to be able to lead.

And let's be clear - I was lucky. I was offered the choice to have my colon *removed* and replaced with a colostomy bag (to which I politely-but-firmly said no), yet some people don't have that option as their condition is much more severe.

I'm happy I made that choice, though, and it set the tone for how I would go on to respond to the illness. I could have taken an easier route and relieved my symptoms instantly, but I did not want to go down that path and take what was readily offered. I needed to find out more. But where would I look for the answers? The internet wasn't as full of information back then, so I started to connect with people and ask for help, *'Hey, so I've got this chronic illness...'* being a great conversation starter. One friend - suffering for years, it turned out, from a similar illness - passed on a book that, without her realizing it, would benefit me in the strangest of ways.

Something immediately shifted on seeing the title of the first chapter: *It's Not Your Fault*. Somehow that didn't feel right. Through the book, I then joined some online forums on colitis (remember forums?!). Although I found a connection quickly, it felt like some of the people I met online were as depressed and accepting of their situation as I had been before I got sick. God knows they had probably been through enough struggle and pain to come to a place of resignation and passivity; it's completely understandable. But the support felt like a crutch to me at that moment, because at that stage, accepting the illness as part of my life and the limitations it imposed on me (medication, fragile energy levels, chronic digestion issues) effectively meant I was always going to be dependent and powerless. This stirred me into action, and I learned one of the most valuable lessons that life has ever given me. I decided to take full responsibility for the situation I now found myself in and to do something about it. Back then, I hadn't added up the limiting beliefs and lifestyle choices I mentioned earlier as factors that I believe contributed to my health problems, so this was a pretty big deal.

To develop inner strength, I believe it is essential we take full ownership of our lives because when we do this, we have the chance to make choices every step of the way. I feel almost silly writing it, and yet I can see from the people I now help that this is often a crucial missed step. Of course, life throws all kinds of things at us that we can't 'control', but how we respond to these events is what defines us, even years later.I could have continued to sit in misery, accepting that I'd always have these symptoms and that there was nothing to be done about it.In saying 'no' to the disease dictating things forevermore, I instead chose to see it as something to work with, and crucially that all this had happened to me for a reason.

I had been woken up with a not-so-graceful slap, and I decided to make some radical shifts in my life as a result. I realized that it was a choice to stay working in the bar...so I quit. It was a choice to be in a relationship, so I left it. Big decisions. But empowering ones. I took things one step further by taking a year off and traveling the world, medication-in-tow. Stepping out like that on my own was again a big deal for me and I experienced real growth. I could write a whole book on my journey and experiences, but suffice to say here that it was one of the greatest years of my life, full of freedom, discovery, fun and connection.

That summer in Sydney, I fell in love and relocated to Nuremberg, Germany, having the desire to continue discovering new things. I started from scratch, learning to teach Business English and finding a calling there. I felt alive and creative and adjusted to life in a new place with a new language. I didn't feel stuck and fearful anymore. Meanwhile, my disease still needed attention… My doctors had given me minimal information about what kind of diet might be safe to follow because it can vary from person to person. So I researched all the diets I could find…and I tried them all. From low-carb to slow-carb to no-carb; from superfood to vegetarian to vegan to fat-adapted. I did the work to see what I could learn about my body and how it responded to these changes. Let me be clear: this was a long process. I kept food diaries and recorded improvements, but to my dismay, just as one kind of food seemed 'safe', I would then react to it. This experimentation and trial-and-error took time, but I never gave up. Step-by-step, I was learning and making tiny improvements along the way, and this allowed me to build my confidence.

Taking care of my health was becoming fun because I saw it as a process without a fixed result at the end - it was not a battle but a form of growth, and I felt like I had been given a chance to live differently. And most importantly, in growth and responsibility, I was also living two of my core values. Could you name your five central core values right now, if someone asked? Knowing and starting to live mine was a game-changer. They were and continue to be: responsibility, honesty, authenticity, integrity, connection and growth. If we are not living from our values, we are out of alignment on some level, affecting many areas of our lives. God knows I wasn't living any of them in the lead up to becoming sick, so it dawned on me that perhaps there was a connection here.

What I was also learning was to cultivate zero attachment to outcome, and this was another essential life lesson. If we attach a specific result or desired outcome to what we do, we might well be disappointed. Suddenly we have hopes and expectations, and wo could be setting ourselves up for failure, which in my mind are dangerous things when trying to improve our health.

The process itself is more important than the outcome. This is true, too, of art, and certainly my experience when writing music, and I wish I'd known this much earlier in life.

In slowly building a relationship with my disease, I had a mutual agreement with my colon; it wouldn't misbehave if I didn't (i.e. no trigger foods like beer, dairy, and bread). The arrangement worked well. I became more sensitive to my body's cues, and I noticed that at the onset of stress, it would give gentle warning signs. I learned to appreciate these instead of fear them - talk about a gut feeling! The body has a wisdom way beyond our own, and it communicates without words. I learned to listen to it; you can call it trusting your intuition if you like. It was making noises and I knew then that things weren't working out in Nuremberg, so I moved up to Hamburg, where I had studied and always felt more at home; and my symptoms calmed down again. When I was happier, I was healthier, I realized.

I was enjoying living in Hamburg; my symptoms were under control; I was thriving at work.... I was even DJ-ing at house parties and the occasional club. Then one day, it occurred to me that maybe I didn't need to be on medication if things were feeling so stable. It was a risk but one worth taking. *What's the worst that could happen if this doesn't work out?* I figured. The medication was a safeguard; I could always go back to it, if needed. It's a choice: stay in my comfort zone or see what's just outside it. And so I came off my medication and have never taken any since. While still a huge victory, this required patience and a new level of awareness and perseverance. If I got stressed, I would feel it instantly in my stomach, another sign that my state of mind had more to do with things than I thought.

After years of looking at Eastern and Western approaches to health, my essential worldview is now this: Western medicine is wonderful and has helped to repair and prolong life, but for me it doesn't do enough to address the root cause of illness. It looks to reduce the symptoms without doing enough to understand *why* the symptoms first appear. Eastern medicine, thousands of years old, like India's Ayurveda (the 'Science of Life') and Traditional Chinese Medicine do things differently, and we're now starting to see a meeting of the western and eastern approaches, as Neuro-Scientific Research, more and more validates ancient wisdom. There is also now a recognition of the part that ancient techniques like yoga, qi gong and meditation, which all harness the power of the mind, have to play in health and wellbeing.

I'll paraphrase if I dare, but what I think they are saying is this: *your sickness is almost always a symptom of a more significant problem, and one that started in the mind.* Today, we know enough about autoimmune diseases to say that they are rooted in inflammation, indeed that 95% of *all* lifestyle illnesses are, and that inflammation is borne of stress. So, treating the symptom is not going to the root of the problem. Sickness means something is out of balance in your life, and the big question is: *Where is the imbalance?* If we can learn to see the imbalance early enough, maybe we don't have to get sick.

Back in Hamburg, my confidence was high off medication. I was in a new relationship and from a new place of stability and balance, I started to look ahead long-term. Another thing missing from my life back in the UK was a clear sense of direction, so I decided to change that step by step. First, I wanted to set a goal of earning €5,000 a month and to take Fridays off. So I stepped out of my comfort zone of working only through language schools and embarked on acquiring corporate clients. It took effort and a lot of rejection, but over time I became very successful, and was easily surpassing my goals. The wind in my sails was of self-belief and determination, built on the work I had done with my illness, and this lasted several years. I discovered surfing in Portugal and was hooked, going there often. I felt unstoppable. The next step was to co-found a language school and translation agency with a business partner, slowly freeing up my days as my passion for teaching faded. I had a clear goal in mind: teach less, grow more.

I wanted to find out more ways to stay balanced and reduce stress, so I dove into self-development, reading countless books as I began to understand myself and my motivations on a much deeper level. Self-acceptance, like everything I've written about here, is not an overnight process. Another life lesson was to learn, again, to ask for help. We're not here to have to figure everything out on our own; it's a fallacy of modern culture and the drive for independence as a way to success is leaving us more and more exposed and isolated when we're wired to connect. This was when I opened myself up to therapy, which I recommend to absolutely everyone.

It was here that I reached a challenging moment as I began to change internally. I wasn't enjoying the weekend nightlife as much and preferred getting up early and going to farmer's markets and *'being all healthy and shit'*, as one friend lazily put it. When you feel a calling in life to do something different, it can and will challenge the people around you, as your behavior starts to question theirs by default. I was feeling a little rejected and isolated, and both these states I feared greatly. But when you know in your heart that you need to go in another direction, I urge you to follow it. There is often a period of isolation, which, if we look at it another way, is transition. *It is sometimes necessary for you to reject your environment if it doesn't serve you anymore, and with it, accept a period of loneliness, letting go and separation.* This is where self-belief, trust and faith are essential. This is how you cultivate real strength.

Deep changes were taking place in my heart and soul, and I was inspired to come back to writing music as a form of creative release, which I did, writing maybe twenty songs over a period.

We are all creative beings, and if you don't think so, I urge you to read *The Artist's Way* by Julie Cameron. It is this book I have to thank above all others. It opened my eyes to synchronicity and reconnected me to a depth of expression I'd forgotten I had. I knew I had to face my first fears finally, and play my music to people. I can't tell you how nervous I was (not only was I playing guitar but I was also singing for the first time), and my friends were just as worried as me!

It was a beautiful evening, and I'm grateful for their grace and presence. Good friends are everything.

And so now to a crossroads, and profound synchronicity.

It's 2016, ten years after I was first diagnosed with Ulcerative Colitis. I've been encouraged to take my music seriously after playing several times and receiving very kind feedback. The music no longer calls me though; those performances have completed their purpose for now at least - I overcame my fear and I sang my most profound truths. I've stopped teaching English too. After almost ten years of teaching language, I realised that I wanted to teach something with more impact, something that inspires me. My

*language school is thriving; I have money in the bank,
I'm safe. I now own a flat in a small town in Portugal
which I'm moving to in a few months. I think I'll be
happy there, surfing and managing my part of the
business online. But I'm still looking for something new.
I hear about a podcast from a friend. I listen to a man
with 26 world records who can sit in ice water for two
hours; doing things science says are impossible, like
controlling his nervous system. I watch an inspiring
documentary where he trains regular folk like you and
me to do the impossible. They walk up a freezing
mountain in nothing but shorts and practise a
groundbreaking breathing technique that is
scientifically proven to reduce inflammation in an
unprecedented way. There is a very affordable online
course, which I sign up for immediately. Intuition is
screaming...this is it!*

I've just discovered the Wim Hof Method.

Although well-known now, back then, Wim was just
starting to make ground in the media outside his
native Netherlands, and as I described these
profound and beautiful experiences I was having -
breathing and taking cold showers essentially - my
friends were skeptical and they laughed at me.
Despite feeling incredible, it was hard. But I was used
to doing things that were different, and was about to
be rewarded for my persistence. After just three
weeks of following the course, I felt a lightness and

strength in my body I had not known for as long as I could remember. Long story short, the method cleared out any residual inflammation in my body and, effectively, my disease with it. To this day, I have had zero symptoms of my illness whatsoever. I can eat whatever I want now that the inflammation is gone. No limits. More than that, my immune system is so strong that I am rarely sick; it's incredible.

I've often talked about how the Wim Hof Method cured my illness, but it's not the complete picture. The reality is that the years of trial and error and learning about my body and mind left me with a drive, resilience, confidence and inner strength that paved the way for the method to do its work, the final piece in my self-healing that I might not have stuck to otherwise. This blessing also happened because I was not attached to any outcome of it curing anything, because of my persistence and commitment to doing it diligently - alone without guidance but pure curiosity - and because of a faith in possibility, based on what I had seen Wim achieve.

I immediately sign up to become an instructor, not realizing I'll be one of the first outside The Netherlands. I'm accepted, and three months after discovering the method, I attend a weekend module with Wim and forty others. I'm accepted onto the master module, scheduled in six months. I train with breath; I train with ice. I am the strongest I've ever been, the healthiest I've ever been. I move to Portugal, saying goodbye to my home and friends of ten years to live the dream life: the four-hour workweek and a lot of surf.

Or so I thought. Looking back, those few lonely months were just another transition. We think we want the beach life, kicking back, sipping cocktails and taking it easy, the end of a journey that made it all worth it. But it didn't last long for me. My addiction to surf was sated, but I was empty. There are six core needs that every human has, and they run in this order: certainty, variety, significance, connection, growth and contribution. The higher up the ladder we go, the more fulfilled we are. The more we can prioritize relationships, our growth, and giving back, the more long-term, sustainable happiness we will have. What are you currently prioritizing, and why? Must it be that way, and how would your life change if you made some shifts?

In those few months, the only need I met was certainty - no wonder I felt so low. I decided that this was not my home, after all. It was neat how everything fell into place. The master module in Poland was around the corner, and was the ultimate test of inner strength I had ever faced...

It's close to 0°C and you're in shorts. You're told to wade into a freezing stream with thirty others and sink in it up to your neck.

And stay there.

Minutes pass. You find balance and calm in the freezing, moving stream as best you can. After close to ten minutes, you're told to come out.

No, this isn't the army, you're paying to do this.

You stand in silence, waiting for instructions. None come. You start to shiver, but try to hide it. Others are doing the same, you can tell. The shivering becomes uncontrollable, like nothing you've ever experienced. Teeth are chattering wildly. Finally, come the instructions, but they are not to try and warm up, they are to let go and shiver as much as you need to. Fear sets in; this is approaching hypothermia and very dangerous. You don't trust what will happen to your body. Precisely, it is explained.

Learn to let go. Have faith and let your body do what it needs to.

The ultimate test for me. Let go and feel the wild, spasmodic shivering…and have faith.

So you do it.

You focus your awareness and trust your intuition….and the shivering stops. You're fine.

Now get back in the water!

You jump in; it's just as cold as before. But this time something's different…you. You scream, jump, laugh, and play with the others.

Now find that place of calm in the water, and step out mindfully.

You do. It's easy now. You're out of the water again. And there's no shivering. You smile and slowly walk back to the house.

This is one of many incredible moments that made five days seem like weeks for all of us. Here I was meeting every need *except* certainty, and I felt so alive! Out there in the freezing nature of the Polish mountains, I had one of the most transformative weeks of my life. Up there, we all felt we were at the start of something big, and so it's proven. The Wim Hof Method has exploded and made breath work and ice baths almost household names alongside mindfulness and meditation. Hundreds of thousands of people have reported its benefits, giving them more energy, better moods, less stress, anxiety and depression, to healing all kinds of serious illnesses.

But remember, don't go in with expectations. The gifts are in exploring the depths of the mind and sticking to the process even if you can't feel it's doing something all the time. In our ever-increasing culture of instant gratification and peak experience-chasing, we are in danger of missing out on the moments of stillness and seeing what is there, beneath the clear lake of the mind. For this awareness and so much more, I have Kasper van der Meulen to thank. Wim is the inspiration and a leader, but Kasper was the teacher, and I invite you to look him up.

The journey is reaching its conclusion...

It's New Years' Eve, 2019. I'm in Rørvig, Denmark, on my silent retreat, writing this piece and meditating in front of fires into the night. After Poland, I moved to Bali for three months, which turned into three years. They feel like ten. Here I've studied yoga, qi gong, meditation, flow states and I facilitate these and other embodiment modalities in workshops alongside the Wim Hof Method, using it as a gateway to help people find balance and inner stillness. I did a workshop tour of Australia, and now teach at leadership programs for an organization in China, and give talks at conferences around the world. What an incredible journey.

I have a thriving coaching business, where I help people reduce stress and find more flow in their lives. I help people trust themselves more, have better relationships and a stronger clarity of purpose in what they're doing. I believe that before we can make effective change, we need to be in a place of alignment, with our values, with what we love doing, and what is natural to us. I'm driven to help people do what I did, to live a life of meaning, to share their strengths and in some way, give back finding an authentic connection with others and the self. This is my purpose. And I still write and play music too. The reason for sharing this story is to show that if I can do these things - a regular, cynical city boy from the south of England - then surely so can you. I hope in these sharings and tools you find some inspiration and something useful; and my deepest wish is that you now take the next step: choose to make a change. And remember...it's about the journey, not the destination. Enjoy the process and your life. Give back as you evolve, and stay in balance as you grow; with yourself, those around you, and your environment. It's all about balance.

"You don't realize how strong you are, until being strong is the only option you have."

~ Unknown

CHAPTER SEVEN

❖

Journey into Timbarra

By Andre Messina

I take this moment to embrace the oneness with the creator spirit...the oneness with the guardians of this earth, water, air & spirit/matter, the ancestors that have walked before me, the great ones emerging, and the ones still to come...

I have walked through many chapters in my life that have served to *train my inner strength.* Each chapter has led me to yet another challenge. As I've completed each task, I have seen them as Divine tests, preparing me for the next. How I have carried myself through each, has determined the next level I would receive.

Like walking through a Labyrinth, I have walked through the valleys of low vibration challenges, in order to reach the next level. Eventually, I have received higher vibratory challenges. Accordingly, the people that have come in and out of my life, I have received as guests sent from the Divine. I have understood that, if I could be open to the ones that were sent, no matter what, I would eventually receive lighter beings, showing I had earned friendship with the earth and its inhabitants.

My relationship with the land began in 2007. My friend, Jan, invited me to his remote property in Tenterfield in the

Northern Tablelands of New South Wales. Jan moved out from Belgium to Australia with his family in 2005. He was an adventurer, someone who made life exciting for himself and for those around him. He invited me to the property on one of our first dates. I felt my heart skip a beat as I drove into the property. There were horses and a beautiful creek flowing through the property, called Quigeram Creek.

This creek flows into the Timbarra —or Rocky—river. First called the Timbarra, but later known as the Rocky, this tract of steep, rugged country lies between the Bulldog Range on the east and the steep rough ranges on the western side. Poverty point. The river rises at Glen Elgin, and flows into the Clarence River at Tabulum, 80 kilometers east of Tenterfield.

The Rocky, once the scene of gold rushes and a goodly number of mainly Chinese miners, is now quiet cattle country, too rugged and dingo-infested for sheep. It is used by some to shelter their cattle in winter from the colder portions of our cold Tenterfield district, while others find it a pleasant place to reside. Roads enter the Rocky through Billirimba and Long Gully, via Drake. Of late, a fire trail from 'The Scrub' provides another entrance when weather permits.

I was looking for a retreat, a place of solace from a competitive world. I had had a lot of trauma as a child, and my soul was looking for healing.

I was the oldest of three young girls who had testified against a man in the High Court for sexual abuse when I was just nine years old.

My parents were both heroin addicts; they were also registered on the methadone program. I lost my mother to a drug overdose when I was sixteen. The years leading up to her death were so lonely! She had started using heroin when I was seven, so from age seven to sixteen, I had no way to communicate with the woman who had birthed me. She was in her own universe and was on a mission to self-destruct.

I was like a deer blinded by headlights! The fear that I was not good enough cut very deep, as my own mother had apparently decided I wasn't worth living for. I overcame the trauma at the time by compartmentalizing it. I had stored it somewhere deep in my psyche, detached from the emotions, as I was too young to process them at the time.

Physically, I would just run, run, run! Literally, I would get out onto the road and run. This seemed to make me feel better. I was also able to find a place of 'no mind' and trained myself to 'soldier on'.

I had managed to survive, but I wasn't living. Nor was I happy. I was a very deep being, with a need to release, restore and regenerate. My inner strength definitely needed to be built up.

After a messy divorce in 2001, all my trauma resurfaced. With no support, and an inability to express my true emotions, I fell into a deep depression. I was using substances to self medicate.

I was incarcerated in 2004 for three months due to this. In prison, I fell to my knees and asked for help from the Divine. I asked for a friend to come into my life. I knew I was a good person, and deserved happiness.

It was only six weeks after I was released that I met Jan. The love of my life. I felt my heart skip a beat when we sat together for a coffee at a café. He had also been through a messy divorce, with his own issues. But he had a gentleness about him that made me feel safe.

I moved my life out of the city to Tenterfield, New South Wales to be with Jan, and we joined forces. Between us, we had five children, so we made a zany Brady bunch— and had a lot of fun together. Our lives became worth living. We had love and we had each other. Jan and I had a weird and wonderful relationship. We really went wild and helped set each other 'free'.

We opened up the property after seven years of idyllic isolation from the world and its craziness. We started with a few dogs, horses and cows. The herds of cows provided no income; in fact, we lost money. This was obviously just for the love of the animals. However, I enjoyed the vibration of the cattle, very sacred animals with sacred mother energies.

In 2007, we decided to grow marijuana to support the farm. This ended badly with me serving seventeen months in prison. It was one of the loneliest times of my life, as my children weren't allowed to contact me. I had wanted to show Jan that I had the spirit of a true warrior. I risked all for this relationship and property.

To build up my inner strength, I spent my time studying spirituality and religion. I wrote heartfelt poems to everyone I loved. It was here that I found a well of love in my heart that I could tap into as I was removed from all distractions from the outer world.

While in jail, I worked as a gardener and cleaner to release any pent-up stress or emotions. I also studied the other women and how they were treated within the system. This gave me unconditional love and compassion for other prisoners.

I have stayed in contact with a few of the women I met on that journey. Every woman had her story. I was no different from any of them, I found. As a collective family of females in a space without men to distract us, I found a lot of time to meditate on the needs and issues of women. I formulated a plan to change the system, should there ever be an opportunity to overhaul the corrective system.

Building up women's inner strength was to be the focus. A Jillaroo school is something we would love to birth down here in the Timbarra hills. One of the best ideas that came through was to get them out into nature, working with the animals and space to process what I had found within myself — trauma, addiction, toxicity from bad diets, and confused minds.

On my release from prison, we adopted German and Belgium shepherd dogs. I have now spent many years with these amazing creatures, and they have been my greatest teachers. They have helped me understand the female is very different from the male of this species. Not just in the obvious ways, but also in the ways they move and communicate. This was an amazing revelation!

Our farm is now a fully licensed dog breeding facility. It's a beautiful way to serve, and we have learned the true nature of unconditional love from these canine sentient beings. We honor them, and they love living in the village we have built for them. I've spent the best part of the last ten years committed to this project.

I have also built up inner strength on this project. I have learned daily discipline, while healing trauma. I have endeavored to give every dog a happy life. The families who have adopted our dogs have also gone through an emotional journey with the adoption. Quite often, they have lost a dog also, so it's been a close connection to the wider community.

It has not been easy for me to ground in life before, so focusing on dogs has been a strong grounding force. The unconditional love they give also provides me solace. The communication with the dogs has taught me a lot about energy, and how to read energy. This has even helped me in my awkwardness with people!

I have had many dreams about one of the Original elders of this land, Lewis Walker, from the Bunjalung mob. He has been like my brother and the dreams of him I've held close to my heart. One night, I dreamed about him. In the dream, a red-bellied black snake slithered into the compound. She had come to inspect to see if we were open and loving towards her grandson. She was a feisty snake who would not be scared off easily. She checked out my whole home, and even went through the artists' space.

Within two hours, Lewis arrived in his little red car and spent a week with my daughter and me! We had the most beautiful week together. He painted a painting for Jan, to show the beauty and colors that he sees the world with.

The elders have different eyes than us. They see things we don't see.

He took me to our water hole and gave me his sunglasses to wear to look at the river. It was magical!

This was his grandmother's spirit. She danced on top of the water in an amazing formation.

I respect and follow the Original people's Star lore and Creation Storytelling. They are magical beings. I am proud to be welcomed into their dreaming. They are one with the earth and have been here living in harmony with Star lore, Bird lore and Bootherum ancient knowledge of all landscape and waterways.

I feel Original customs and ceremonies are important to understand if we want to continue calling this Earth our home. I feel very connected to the ancestral spirits of this land, Mother Earth. I feel that the Earth and I are one. We have both been through storms, drought, abundance, lack, and rest and restoration. I am her, and she is me.

The year 2019 has been the worst drought in history on this land, Australia. As I type, there are many fires burning this land. They started in my town, Tenterfield, in September 2019. The waterways are depleted, and many homes, people and animals have been lost. My fellow tribesmen have confirmed that this is karmic. This is a process we are going through; purification, realization, building inner strength, and connection with the original people is an important step forward.

They explained to me that the massacres that have happened in this country have created a low karmic energy. Some of the towns are very depressed. There is a lot of struggle within the working class of Australia. Poverty and addictions are rife. Depression is the word I would use for this period. It's like repressed energy that hasn't been expressed. Everyone is lethargic and listless. The farmers don't have much happiness; they are struggling. There is a high suicide rate amongst the young, especially the indigenous.

June 2019, I decided to go on a walkabout with one of the Gidabul elders and another woman named Nicole. I had been living at the property for thirteen years, and never been on a proper walkabout! I had to see this wonderful country, Australia! I knew that this was a rite of passage to build up my inner strength. Living in my car, with no home, living from day to day, and visiting tribal mob.

I spent many weeks with elder YDO and Nicole on the walkabout. We talked, we laughed, and we healed together.YDO was carrying much trauma from his life as a full-blood original elder. He had been imprisoned and suffered much oppression and trauma. He had been one of the *Black Panthers*, a vigilante group that would ride trains and keep the young people in line. The Maori and Original tribes had a lot in common, we found. We were connecting. We were family!

Nicole and I were two mothers who had always lived for others. Husbands, children, social expectations, and expected roles. We had hardly given ourselves any time or passion for our own lives. This was a new, exciting venture for the both of us. We weren't just doing this for us. This was women's business!

Sometime during the trip, Elder YDO had stated, "You are both mothers breaking the waters, ready for the birthing to come." What did this mean? I wondered. Were we paving the way for more women to break out of their stereotypical lives? Or was this the beginning of the movement of the Original people? Was there going to be a birthing? This was an amazing moment for Nicole and me!

The first Camp we visited was at Bowen, Far North Queensland. I was surprised to see, that it was the 'Anti Adani' camp. A secret location of Earth's Warriors. The people who camped there were front-line activists, protesting at the Indian Company for buying up land and getting licenses to tap into the Artesian Basin for their mining company.

These people had left their homes, families and jobs to chain themselves to machinery; to protest against this foreign company and the potential sites of the mining. It was a makeshift camp, but seemed to run quite well, with media rooms, kitchen, and gardens backing onto the dry riverbed. This was an exciting place for anyone wanting to feel support and become active in what has been happening to our land.

Every morning we would meet and discuss the running of the camp, any jobs that needed helpers, and what the next activism movement would be. Before every meeting, they would honor the tribal guardians of the land the camp was on, Birri Country and Tribe. The ancestors, and the emerging tribe.

Just down the road lived a Birri Country Sovereign family. They had refused the system and Government support. They had home-schooled their children and created income by producing the most beautiful Aboriginal art, with their own Art studio and creation space on the land. When you arrived at Ken and Maria's property, you were met by signs and artworks showing sovereignty and welcoming you to Birri country.

We were welcomed to sit around the fire. This beautiful family was fighting to protect their tribal land and waterways, as well as tribal burial grounds that were being disturbed by the greed of the Government and Corporations. Families were fighting for the land and the water.

As the Bogie River was dry, I camped right in the riverbed. I set up my little temple, and spent a week praying and connecting with this amazing river tribe. Many rivers were dry, and wildlife was disappearing.

I felt a connection between the indigenous, the weather, and the lack of water.

Further into our journey, we drove into Alice Springs, NT. I felt something land on my shoulder, it was my Mothers spirit! I had never felt her presence so much as then. This time, she was in the image of Kuan Yin, the female Buddha.

Just afterward, we stopped to camp just outside Alice Springs. Out of nowhere, YDO was taken over by an angry spirit! He was angry at my friend, Nicole. She received this angry man's energy without responding. He was channeling all of the oppression of the men of that region, it seemed. It was very intense. I felt for her, but I felt protected by Kuan Yin, my Mother.

YDO had spoken to a friend afterwards about this rage, "I sometimes got very angry at those two women, but, you see, we now have so many diseases and trauma to release." I was filled with empathy for this beautiful elder, at his honesty and his suffering. I was happy to be that sounding board for him. I loved him. It is very apparent though that this anger, and sacred rage, must be expressed to heal. I wondered if a collective space could be arranged, where these broken warriors could heal their wounds with loving women supporting them. It aligned with the dreaming of bringing women together, and then to bring the warriors home to their love and light within them.

Uluru rock is sacred to the Anangu people. I spent the day at this magnificent rock on 17 July 2019, my Mother's birthday. She had passed away when I was sixteen, so I embraced this moment. I never climbed the rock. I respected the wishes of the local tribe, and I only walked around the base of the rock. Very sacred dreaming; I stopped and paused at the spot where the women's ceremonies were held. I could hear the chanting of the women. They were calling me.

Almost thirty-four years to the day, Anangu traditional owners were handed back the title to Uluru. Their wishes that people should not climb the sacred rock would be enforced by law. This has opened up a portal of healing and respecting sacred sites for the rest of the original tribes.

I have met YDO's nephew of the same tribe, Ally Bulligan (Bulligan means 'Strong Beautiful Warrior') He is the Lore keeper. His dreaming has been handed down to him from his Grandmother. He radiates love, fun, and guidance of the Gidabul people. He has a story-- a dreaming story of creation. This is a tribe that honors birds. Ally Bulligan's bird name is 'Black Swan' (Grace). He has connections with my tribe.

Ally Bulligan has also informed me that the dreaming on their land has certain laws, that even their own brothers are unknowingly breaking. For example, it is forbidden to play didgeridoo on their land. Many brothers are playing didgeridoo and even earning a living from this. Our message is to help get the lore of the land corrected so that there can be balance.

I also now have a bird name, 'Black Crow' (Wargahn). I am proud to be part of this amazing tribal culture! We love our land, our earth, our waterways, our birds, and our animals. We are here for the healing. I have heard many stories now. Original creation in its dreaming story. Many have not got the story right.

I am proud to be part of this great earth family. I am a student now, listening, learning, and changing my ways of old. Honoring the elders, helping where needed. My personal life is no longer personal. It is becoming tribal, collective, and one of many. I have integrated. This is a very important process in the building up of my inner strength.

When Jan and I opened up the farm to the youth of the world, we knew it was unheard of; an experiment at the social level of progress. We knew we would be opening something more than the gate and our hearts. This was a portal! The people that have poured through our gates since then have been the most colorful people that this world has created. All different skin colors, religions, likes and dislikes. With one common unity, this thing called *love*.

There is a re-connection needed of the story and the sacredness of this land, with the original beings that have opened up their land, their homes, and their hearts to us all!

The dog-breeding facility has gone through many changes in the ten years I have been present. It started with Jan and me. Then David came along. Now Carolina and a few other people have also helped out over the years. The dog world is a collective energy, just as with cows or sheep, horses. Many dogs have come and gone. I have seen my journey with the dogs as one of service.

I serve them as Gods. In some way, I have felt this would balance the karma that humans and dogs need to rebalance. Every animal has a story line and dreamtime like the original people. It is necessary to heal and create beautiful new dreaming for them, as these stories walk through history (their story) with us. Don't lose the dreaming! If love is guiding and our hearts are leading, then we, and our animals will flourish.

Can we use our relationships with animals, the indigenous and our roles as Earth Shepherds as an example to create a healthy humanity? The fires and drought in our 'Lucky Country', Australia, is more than is seen on the physical plane. Building up inner strength during drought is extremely difficult, but it is possible if we can meditate daily on love and imagine seeing the water flowing around us again.

The animals have left us with so many thoughts; their spirits are with us.

Thankfully, slowly, in December 2019, the rains came, and our beautiful creek is fully flowing with water again! Our patience, diligence, and quietly accepting the dry, has led us to receiving the well-needed rain, and finding our inner strength, individually and communally.

"Strength does not come from winning. Your struggles develop your strengths. When you go through hardships and decide not to surrender, that is strength."

~ Mahatma Gandhi

CHAPTER EIGHT

❖

Igniting, Appreciating and Giving

By Eric Tan

I was both honored and skeptical when asked to be a part of this project. I was honored because I had the opportunity to contribute to this book, alongside the other magnificent authors. Skeptical, because I was just an average 35-year-old guy, living in Singapore. There was pretty much nothing that I could share that might interest or inspire people (at least, that is what I initially thought). Then, I remembered the advice I've given to others.

As a Toastmaster for the past five years, I often have younger members asking me to advise them on what kind of topic they should select as their first speech. I suggest to them to simply share something about themselves. While they may object that their life is not that interesting, I encourage them by saying, "What seems insignificant to you may be significant to one of your audience." Therefore, I decided to take my own advice.

Indeed, I strongly believe because everybody has a story to share. In this journey called life, there will be ups and downs, triumphs, and tribulations. These are life's lessons. We learn both from when we are up and triumphant, as well as when we are down and in tribulation.

This is my story and my journey to riches. I do not know if my chapter will intrigue you, if my stories will impact you, or if my journey will inspire you. I do

know that through writing this chapter, I have realized just how much inner strength I have developed in this journey of riches. So, here's my journey.

PART 1

Who Am I?

**"Unless we based our sense of identity
upon the truth of who we are, it is
impossible to attain true happiness."**

~ Brenda Shoshanna

Who am I? My name is Eric Tan. I am just an average of 35-year-old Singaporean Chinese.

I grew up in a middle-income family, an only child who had undergone 12 years of Singapore's education system before serving two years in the military. After that, I graduated from the National Technological University, Electrical and Electronics Engineering faculty.

After graduation, I started working as an insurance agent for a year and a half before migrating to one of the top companies in Singapore as a Financial Services Consultant. As it is, this has been my first and final career so far. Based on my above description, you might assume that I have been on a smooth journey.

However, every journey possesses its challenges and obstacles. This is the fine print of embarking on this journey. This, my friend, is life.

I have been no exception. In my journey, I too have faced various challenges. These obstacles have required me to dig deep and muster my inner strength to overcome them one at a time and carry on. It has been by no means easy, and I am proud to have been able to overcome all challenges thus far.

The lowest point of my life hit in 2013. My dad passed away. I can still recall that vivid day. It was the fourth day of the Chinese New Year. As I was having a reunion lunch with my then boss and colleagues, my mother called to say my dad had been taken to the hospital and he wasn't breathing.

Without hesitating, I rushed to the hospital, praying that everything would be ok. We waited outside the surgery room, where minutes seemed like hours. Finally, the surgeon came out; got down on one knee, holding my mother's hand and told her they had done their best.

The worst had happened. Everything was so sudden. There were no parting words. There were no goodbyes. He was gone, taken from us by cardiac arrest.

The next few days were torturous. With the Chinese customs, closure did not come immediately; it was a long three-day process. The first day after my father's death, I was asked to visit the coroner's office so that the coroner could verify the death was natural, and no autopsy would need to be conducted. While waiting, I was exceptionally calm, as if it was just another day. I really appreciated having my great buddy, JY, there for me on that day and the following few days. I will always be indebted to him.

Afterward, I was driving to the funeral parlor when the torrent of emotions hit. It was also raining heavily outside as if the heavens felt my pain. Every single memory of our shared experiences flashed before me and I just wailed. I cried the hardest I had ever cried in my entire life, alone in the car, driving in the pouring rain.

By the time I reached my destination, I had experienced an epiphany. I had to be strong for my mother. I knew that the weight of taking care of the family now fell on my shoulders. Most importantly, I knew I could not let my father down.

The moment of grief passed as I told myself, "Dad will always be with me. His blood is coursing through my veins and I will be his greatest legacy." That is how I was able to pick myself up. I made a choice, or rather, I felt compelled to choose because dwelling in sorrow just was not an option. Life had to go on.

Since then, I have made many transitions in my life, especially professionally. I am especially grateful to Mr. Justin Leow, my financial services director for believing in my potential and Mr. Anthony Goh, my direct manager, who selflessly taught me everything that I aspired to know to help me excel in my career.

I was also fortunate enough to meet two talented people who helped change my life for the better. They were Ms. Zhuo Shuzhen and Mr. Oh Chengkok. Because of them both, I was able to join my company's Toastmasters club. That was a life-changing moment.

Toastmasters empowered me to be a better leader, communicator and, most importantly, a better person. Of course, my Toastmasters journey has had its own set of challenges as well; there have been disputes, there have been conflicts, but amazingly, there has always been reconciliation and resolution.

The Toastmasters platform gave me so many opportunities to give speeches and conduct trainings for people from all walks of life, in various community clubs as well as in multi-national corporations. I also applied those skills in my profession. As a result, I have been honored with several prestigious awards in my company over the past few years. I met John Spender through Toastmasters and received this excellent opportunity to contribute to this book. Most importantly, I found my soulmate, Arisa, because of Toastmasters.

You can say that I am at the prime of my life. I have been to the valley of darkness and I am now at the top of the mountain. I have been able to muster inner strengths that I did not know that I had until I made the transition.

It is only at this point in my life that I can verbalize my inner strengths and share them with you. While I do not expect what I share will pose any impact on you, I believe that if at least one reader out there is enlightened by this chapter, that will be my most significant highlight. Let's get right to it.

PART 2

Inner Strength #1:
Ignite Your Fighting Spirit

**"Life is a matter of Choices and every
choice you make makes you."**

~ John. C. Maxwell

When I began my career in insurance, I knew that it
was going to be a journey filled with rocks and
pebbles. Rejection comes with the remuneration. I
had my fair share of rejections. By my 8th year in the
business, I thought that I was immune to them, but I
was wrong.

In 2017, I had a rare opportunity to help a customer
secure a S$3 million insurance plan to protect his
assets. I knew very well what the significance of this
deal held for me. There would be recognition and
remuneration, especially for a young advisor. I was
naive enough to believe that this was all I should
strive for in life. How wrong I was, and thankfully, this
experience and this client helped me realize there
was more to life. I was eternally grateful to him!

Everything was going smoothly. The client had
accepted my pitch; my manager and I even saved
another S$30,000 through numerous negotiations with

my company. We were so confident that we would secure this deal! And yet, the client pulled the plug because his wife, whom I hadn't met in the whole process, had other plans. His reason for me was simple.

"A Happy Wife is a Happy Life."

Seven simple words shattered my deal. The three months preparation and the cruise that I was supposed to go on, were all in vain. I was utterly disappointed. The deal that can potentially take me to the next level in my career disintegrated right before me. I applied my experience to convince the client to reconsider, but it was futile.

After recognizing it was over, I suddenly felt lost and helpless. I made a beeline to my sanctuary, the library, the place where all the wisdom in the world gathered, the place where I felt baptized with quietness. I found one seat at the corner and I just sat there, staring into space, thinking, "What have I done wrong? What else can I do to remedy the situation?"

After what seemed like hours, I started to ask myself more questions. *Do I feel angry?* Yes. *Do I feel disappointed?* Yes. *Do I feel sad?* Yes. Do I want to continue feeling this way? NO!"

I refused to be defeated by this setback, and drowned in my sorrow. I needed to get back on the saddle. I did three things that I found immensely useful that I still apply to this day.

1. Talk to Somebody

I texted my co-workers' in our group-chat that I didn't secure the deal. Within minutes, texts full of encouragement started pouring in. "Stay positive, Eric, there will be another deal." "Some things in life we cannot control, you did your best, that's all that matters." All the support and encouragement comforted me and made me feel I wasn't alone.

Thus, speaking to someone, whoever it may be, is helpful.

2. Acknowledge Your Emotional State.

Disappointment and dejection can be an abyss that just sucks you in and keeps you spiraling down. However, we all have an innate trait where, when push comes to shove, we will retaliate. All of us have the fighting spirit, but to ignite it, you need to first acknowledge your current emotional state.

That was what I did. What I told myself back then was, "Yes, I am angry. Yes, I am disappointed. Yes, I am Sad..."

Now in hindsight, I realize that it is highly essential to acknowledge your current emotional state. You can tell yourself to move on and be positive a hundred times, but if you stop being honest to yourself, your mind will believe that those words of encouragement you gave yourself are mere facades to hide your real emotions. It is through acknowledgment that you can de-clutter and expunge the negativities that are in your system, and ignite your fighting spirit.

3. Ignite Your Fighting Spirit

Yes, I am angry. Yes, I am disappointed. Yes, I am sad, *but I will not give up!*

I recognized every single one of my emotions. I knew how I was feeling and most importantly, I understood why I was feeling that way. The final question I asked myself is, "What's Next? Giving up is not an option; if I wanted to give up, I would have quit long ago."

Since giving up is not an option, then the only way to fight back is by moving on. Moving on is not about just leaving without taking anything away with you. Instead, you should be like an anthropologist to excavate, extract and examine what the key takeaways are to empower you for similar potential obstacles in the future. This is one of the reasons we studied history, to learn from our past to shape the present, as we progress to the future.

I made it a point to remember all the invaluable lessons that I could garner from this experience and move on. An interesting thing happened after I did that. In my subsequent appointments with customers (both potential and current), I was able to secure more deals because I had learned from this one experience, applying the lessons to my subsequent contracts even up till today.

I learned two valuable lessons from this experience.

Firstly, we always have a choice to be happy and we still have an opportunity to rebound in the face of setbacks -- to recognize that it is not difficult to make a choice. Again, we must first be honest with ourselves. This clarity will help us tremendously in our journey of riches.

Secondly, what appears to be a setback may in hindsight, be a learning experience for us to be better. We can see every delay as a steppingstone to our future success.

These three steps are akin to training in the gym. We all know that to build our health and strength, we too need to adopt the above methods: Firstly, have a spotter to help you push beyond your limits at moments when you think you will give up. Secondly, recognize your strengths and limitations to prevent unnecessary injuries. Finally, never give up and keep pushing yourself to your limit.

Similarly, to develop your inner strength, the same principles apply. Firstly, talk to someone (just like having a spotter). Next, acknowledge your emotional state (knowing your strength). Finally, ignite your fighting spirit (keep pushing yourself).

The key is the same as going to the gym, to do it consistently and continuously. With that, you will be able to muster up your inner strength when your chips are down or when your back is against the wall, to get you through any life's obstacles.

PART 3

Inner Strength #2:
Appreciate What You Have

"Trade your expectations for appreciation and the world changes for you."

~ Anthony Robbins

A primary school teacher was writing the multiplication table on the board.

9 x 1 = 9
9 x 2 = 18
9 x 3 = 27
.
.
.
9 x 10 = 9

Suddenly many students raised their hands and exclaimed, "Teacher, teacher, you got the last line wrong. It should be 90." The teacher smiled and replied, "Yes, it is, but I got it right for the first nine times, why didn't anyone of you commend me?" Indeed, we often find ourselves focusing on the black dot on a piece of white paper instead of focusing on the rest of the white.

There was a time when I was continually chasing the next targets. Some may say that this is because I had a sales-based career, which always required that. Even when I achieved my targets, I felt that the sense of happiness didn't seem to last. The chase gave a hit of dopamine that made me feel like an addict seeking the next fix.

Then, I was blessed to meet the love of my life!

Arisa is a beautiful and incredible lady from the land of smiles, Thailand, who brings out the best in me. She has a heart filled with compassion, kindness, and love. She works in Singapore and even though she does not earn a lot, she has used her savings to help rebuild her family's house back in their village so that they could have much better living conditions. It was she, who taught me that true happiness comes not from getting what we do not have but from appreciating what we already have.

Arisa recommended I watch a YouTube program broadcast from Thailand. The name of the show was "Super 10". It was a talent show where children under the age of 15 displayed their talent. In return, they would be able to fulfill one of their wishes. One night, I was watching this program and the episode impacted me to this day. An eleven-year-old boy from one of the rural provinces of Thailand participated. His parents had separated when he was very young, and he was brought up by his aging grandparents. The place he lived is something that a city boy like me could NEVER imagine. The roof of the place was dilapidated, and this boy and his grandparents slept on the hard wooden floor.

When the show's host asked him what his wish was, he simply said: "I hope to get a mattress for my grandparents to sleep on." A mattress? So simple an item most of us would take for granted, but that was all that this boy wished for – and for his Grandparents. Throughout the entire show, the boy seldom smiled as he performed. He was good at a sport called Petanque. He was so good that one of the judges commented that the National Petanque Association in Thailand should get to know the boy.

I could not help but notice through the entire show, the boy seldom smiled. It was as if the weight of the world rested on his shoulders. He only broke into a smile after his talent was recognized by the audience and the panel of judges – and after he knew that he had successfully helped his grandparents receive the mattress they deserved. In the end, he looked directly at the camera and expressed his thanks to his aging grandparents.

I will remember that scene for the rest of my life. That level of gratitude is indescribable.

From just this one episode and through my soulmate, I began to take stock of what I had: an apartment with a comfy bed; a decent car; a great career; a beautiful family; and a precious soulmate. I realized that I had absolutely no reason not to be happy, nor did I have the excuse to beat myself up when I met any setbacks.

In the journey of riches, you will gain some and you will lose some, but the question is, will you appreciate what you have learned, or will you continue to lament what you missed? Mr. Anthony Robbins said it best, "Trade your expectations into appreciation and the world changes for you." Cherish everything you have, *especially* the people around you because they are your inner strength.

Building and appreciating your strong support group gives you confidence and the inner strength you need to fight against all odds and emerge victorious in life's battles. By doing so, you will be able to wake up every day with positive energy. Once this energy courses through you, no problem will be so immense that it can't be solved. Appreciating what you have is a superpower. Use It!

PART 4

Inner Strength #3:
ThePower to Give

**"We make a living by what we get;
we make a life by what we give."**

~ Winston Churchill

All of us have the power of giving, but many feel that giving is an act that only the rich and famous ought to do. In my opinion, there is nothing more valuable and precious than to give or impart a skill, knowledge, or experience to another. There is a saying that I passionately believe that goes like this, "Give a man a fish, he will thank you for a day; teach a man to fish, he will thank you for a life time."

This is reiterated in Simon Sinek's book of *Leaders Eat Last*, where he mentioned the four chemicals, Endorphin, Dopamine, Serotonin and Oxytocin, and how Oxytocin will course through our system, making us feel good and happy when we help someone.

In my case, I am deeply convinced that when we have our backs against the wall (or so we think), we should give, share, and impart our thoughts, values, and experiences to others. It not only helps others, but it helps us too.

Many people asked me why I joined the Toastmasters community. I could provide them an answer, but if you were to ask me why I am *still* in the Toastmasters organization, I could tell you without skipping a beat that this community provides me a platform to give, to share and to impart. It is just like what my predecessors in the community had done for me.

Whenever I am down, or I feel vexed about work, I make a beeline to a Toastmasters club. The reason is that the members share so generously on their expertise and experience in various subjects and instances in their lives through their speeches. I have been able to draw positive energy through them and I always find myself walking out of a Toastmasters meeting feeling recharged and rejuvenated.

"Practice doesn't make one perfect, for no one is perfect, but practice does make one progress." This is what I learned from one of my mentors, the Distinguished Toastmaster John Sih. That is precisely what I did. I started giving speeches, then progressed to providing workshops and becoming a trainer to train many club officers. I found that the more I shared with others, the more I could apply what I preached in my own professional practice.

The best way to help yourself is to help others. This is another method for me to muster inner strength. Through helping others, I feel empowered that I can resolve or conquer any situation that is blocking my way. That feeling of empowerment is a form of inner strength that I feel can be cultivated only by giving.

One of the most precious things that you can give is your time. I do not know how many of us are struggling with the concept of work-life balance, or if we are too "busy" chasing our dreams that we forget to give time to the people closest to us, to people we care about and of course to the people we love.

I have interacted with many people throughout my life and the discussion about maximizing time has often come up. I have often heard my friends lament that they do not have enough time. At times, I have been guilty of this myself.

Nevertheless, at this point in my life, I believe that the best way to maximize time (if there is such a thing) is essentially simple. Set up a timetable. Have clarity of what it is you need to do at each time of the day. For example, how many hours will you work? How many hours shall you spend with your loved ones? How many hours will you give yourself to read or to exercise?

I find that once I establish this timetable, it provides me a sense of clarity over what I need to do at what time, and during what time interval. It allows me to be present and focus 100%. Once the time is up, you should move to the next activity. The worst thing would be extending your work time to your family time.

Both examples I shared above are not mutually exclusive. I have learned that, if you want to make a difference in your, or someone's else life through sharing, you need to invest your time. That is what I have done. For the past few years, I have found a way to distribute my time evenly between my profession, my self-development, my Toastmasters activities and, of course, spending time with my loved ones.

I have had the blessing to share my beliefs, knowledge, and experience with hundreds of people. The interesting thing is after every sharing, I have honestly felt more positive, more empowered, and more encouraged. This positivity, empowerment, and encouragement have helped me realize how fortunate I was, appreciate the things I had and allowed me to face and take on my day-to-day challenges more courageously.

This, my friend, is the power of giving.

PART #5

The Riches Lie in The Journey

"Wealth is not about having a lot of money; it is about having a lot of options."

~ Chris Rock

Many people in this world spend a lot of time chasing after riches. They make money as their end goal, their destination, but they fail to realize that the riches lie in the journey.

Every journey has an end. The end is simple, fleeting and in the case of most humans, unimpressive. From the moment we are born, we know for a fact where the end of our journey will be, DEATH. We can have millions and billions worth of riches, but in the end, we cannot take a dime away. The only thing that will be with us at our final moment are the memories of the process, the roller-coaster ride, the *journey*.

At various stages of our lives, we will have the options to choose which journey we want to embark on. The moment the decision is made; this decision will shape our lives. Being 35 this year, at the prime of my life, I recognize that I have many things to be thankful for at this moment. I am especially grateful for the life lessons I have learned the hard way. The reason is that all of these life lessons have made me who I am today.

It is through these lessons that I learned to appreciate everything that I have, especially my loved ones, who have supported me unconditionally all these years. It is through these lessons that I know my purpose in this world, and this brings me hope and joy towards the future. It is also through these life lessons that I know that I always have the option to be positive. One way I can achieve this is by surrounding myself with other positive people.

I am sure you can do it too. Whenever you feel you are down in the doldrums or when you think that you are stuck at a crossroads, just remember how far you have come to this current stage and how many obstacles you have overcome to be where you are right at this moment. Your inner strength comes from paying attention to how good you already are and how much you have improved as the years have passed.

I am an ordinary person just like you. We all have our unique issues, but if we reflect upon our lives up till this date, we should be proud of ourselves for overcoming all the trials and tribulations that have tried to bring us down. Yet, we are still standing today in triumph. The strength we have gathered in our lifetime to overcome challenges comes from the people around us, the environment that we are in and, most importantly, the reciprocal effects of our actions.

I always remember four phrases that I heard once in a US presidential rally and I have tweaked it a little to make it my motto:

> **"Be the best that we can. Help as many as we can. Cherish all that we can, for as long as we can."**

My final words of encouragement to you are to relish and enjoy your journey, for the riches are in the journey itself.

"You have power over your mind not outside events. Realize this, and you will find strength."

~ Marcus Aurelius

.

CHAPTER NINE

❖

Alchemize Your Obstacles And Purify Your Body

By Alexandra Cousins

I just knew I had to get out of there! My body had grown weaker and weaker over the course of three days. It was as if someone had opened a valve and all of my life force was seeping out of me. Finding it hard to concentrate, I soon became dizzy and weak. Aside from this, there were no physical symptoms that I could associate with what was happening to me.

One moment I'd be back to normal, finding that a strong coffee was helpful but only temporarily, before I was again overcome by what felt like a fog of confusion. There was a thin veil between what was real and what was not real in those moments. Nothing seemed to make sense. Then there were moments of flashing lights and a buzzing noise that surrounded me.

There was hype around our $25,000 crocodile skin handbags. My whole life, I had dreamt of working in fashion and making a name for myself. I loved creating, and I had landed the perfect opportunity to create a luxury accessory label out of Africa.

We had just made it to the big trade shows in Paris. The money was coming in, and I was having the time of my life. I knew I wasn't going to do this forever. This was just a stepping-stone so that I could eventually do what I wanted to do.

I was the Creative Director of the company. Very proudly, I held this title that I had worked so hard to earn—now realizing that it was all a joke! As I took one last look around the packed room at the Park Hyatt conference centre, my whole body began to pulsate. The familiar yet unwanted feeling of confusion and refracted light began to come and go. My mind kept telling me to get out of there.

Attempts at trying to make sense of what was happening to me were futile. I needed to trust myself. I needed to trust my mind and my body, which were urging me to leave that place. I mumbled to my boss. Slurred words and fatigue tumbled from my lips trying to inform her that I needed to lie down—at that moment—not caring if she would approve. I needed to get out of there. I needed to lie down. I was not feeling well.

For a fleeting moment, I felt like I was running for my life. Up until that point, I had spent my whole life dreaming of working in fashion. I wanted to make a name for myself. My love for creating and the drive to achieve my dreams helped to push me further. I was finally accomplishing what I had always wanted.

These were the best days of my life; or so I thought.

There was beautiful chaos in Paris during Fashion Week. The smell of perfume, cigarette smoke, and espresso filled the air. There were bright colours and beautiful, stylish people as far as the eyes could see. Most of the people seemed to be of great importance, holding their heads high and strutting around in style. They had a charisma and confidence that most people envied.

It was my dream to belong among them, to assimilate into their lifestyle and to reside in their world. I wanted to play like them, move like them, be like them. I felt like I was almost there, only to be overwhelmed by a strangeness that was taking over my body, something I could barely describe in logical words. What was wrong with me?

Panting across the streets of the fashion capital of the world, all I could think of was getting to my room and lying down. I knew trying to get a taxi was futile, and the idea of standing and waiting seemed unbearable.

As I walked around in a fog, I wished I had never gotten myself into this situation. This was not like me. I felt like my strength was dwindling. Cold and hot sweat was pouring down my face, and my knees felt like they would give way any second.

There were so many questions moving in and out of my mind. Should I call an ambulance? Should I ask for help? Should I call my husband? If I did call, what would I tell him? I wondered what to do as I tried to make sense of everything in my mind.

I thought maybe I should stop and eat something, hoping that it might help, but was not convinced that it would. The unbearable chatter would not quit!"Just walk faster, don't think so much, just walk faster, you can make it to the room and all will be fine; just make it to the room."

There was an uncomfortable chill in Paris. The frostbite and cold wind against my cheeks somehow kept me going. Walking through narrow allies to get to my hotel, I could not stand looking at one more fashion window. I did not want to see one more thing. It was all too much.

Keeping my focus, I hurried, trying to make it to my hotel room. Meanwhile, intrusive thoughts filled my head. *Maybe you are making all of this up. Maybe there is nothing wrong with you. Maybe you are just lazy. Maybe you are just not cut out for this business. Maybe you were a fraud all along. You were a fraud all along; just admit it.* The harsh voices were loud and obnoxious. They were relentless.

I could see the door as I approached. "Almost there," I told myself. Finally, at the door to my hotel! I stumbled inside in a daze. I just needed to make it to my room. Almost there; almost there.

Once inside my room, I ripped my clothes and jewellery off and just collapsed on the bed, still unsure of whether to call an ambulance or not. What would I tell them? I could not move one more finger. I just lay there thinking that, if this was the end of the road for me, maybe I deserved it.

My body felt like a ton of bricks. I could not move. I could barely breathe, and I could not get out of that state. I felt like I was in a coma. I experienced an uncomfortable stillness as I lay there in thought. At least my mind had not yet failed me.

Maybe this is what death feels like.

I had no energy even to continue to think about what was happening to me. I simply did not care anymore. An uncanny silence fell over me—a bliss. There was a nothingness that was sudden and unshakeable. I seemed to become one with all of existence, no longer an individual...Time no longer mattered. Then a voice began to speak to me.

"If you don't stop right now, you will die."

"You are not living your truth and you know it. We have entertained your games for long enough. This is not what you came here for and it is time to stop."

"But I am doing so well; I am making great money and finally I am creating something of value and prestige. I only want to do this one or two more years, and then I'll stop, I promise. Please, can't we make a deal?" I countered.

"No. You must get out now, or you will die. You have weakened your body by living out of alignment with your highest truth, and if you don't stop and focus on coming into full alignment, you will die and you know it."

I did know it. I knew that this was not my purpose. I had always known that I was here for something more significant. I believed I was only using this as a stepping-stone. Then I realized that, although we have free will, when Spirit requires us to step into our purpose, it cannot wait.

As much as there was the part of me that felt all the pressure to "make it"—to be successful, to make my parents proud, to build something, to be somebody—none of it made sense to me on a soul level.

The voice continued: "It's time to trust your Divine essence. I know it is scary, and I know that right now nothing makes sense and it all seems overwhelming, but please understand that We've got you." It was time to listen.

Spirit was continuing. "We've allowed you this time to play so that you could learn that feeding the ego is never truly satisfying. There is more. So much more. And we know it is what you came for. It's time to live it."

"Okay, but how am I going to make money? Money is real and right now I make more than half of our income, and I know that there is no way we can live without it. It's just impossible! So, as much as I agree that I am not living in full alignment, I just need a bit of time. One more year will be enough, I know it!" I pleaded.

"If you don't stop now, you will die! You must withdraw your energies from this project now, or you will die. What you are doing is in such radical misalignment with who you know yourself to be, and your soul will not accept another moment of it. It is appalling that you have let it go this far. Yet we knew it needed to come this way for you to wake up! You have great work to do, but first it starts with yourself."

I wished I could pretend not to know what they were talking about. I swirled many thoughts and possibilities around in my head, as I lay there catatonic.

I knew that no one could help me. No ambulance. No husband. No healer or guru. This was between my spirit guide and me.

As long as I wasn't moving, I felt so good, realising that I was being healed and energetically prepared to recover. I had been in a similar situation several times before; this was home. This was an uncomfortable welcome back to Spirit. It was uncomfortable only because I had veered so far from it. I was able to recognise that this energy was my home. My heart chakra opened and all other chakras settled.

I knew there was only one thing to do: to listen and obey.

You see, many years before, I was reading *The Celestine Prophecy* on a glorious Sunday morning, overlooking Lake Lugano in my hometown in Italy. In the book, James Redfield outlined that we could either chose to live our life from ego and mind, or we could live it fully guided and trusting Spirit. Then, by doing so, we'd become co-creators of the divine.

Up until then, I had zero consciousness, no concept of the idea of co-creating being a possibility. A light bulb came on. My heart opened with excitement and delight, as I had just been given the news that I had been waiting for my whole life!

I put the book down and the whole world looked different.

The forest in front of me shimmered and breathed with me. The lake became a golden portal enlightened by the early morning summer sun. I closed my eyes to take it all in. The world seemed different, brighter and more meaningful. There was Magic. "Magic is real," I said to myself.

I knew then that life was not just about fitting in, doing what we're supposed to do, following the rules, or checking off all of the boxes. I knew—or, rather, remembered—that there wasn't just magic in this life, but that I came here to Be Magic.

I opened my eyes and looked at the glistening lake and, with my gaze, followed the gold ray to the sun. I opened my arms wide and felt the glimmer of gold enter my chest and warm my third eye.

"I commit to living my life led by Spirit. I give full permission to be fully guided by the force that brought me here and to becoming a co-creator with the Divine."

I felt overcome by a deep sense of peace and joy, and I knew at that moment my whole life was about to change radically. I had summoned the courage to live my dreams wholeheartedly. Then I began traveling the world, following my heart and Spirit, which led me to Africa. I planted roots in South Africa, where my great awakenings took place.

I was shown that I am here to create a completely new way of living and that I was to bring the teachings out into the world and create communities. At the time, the vision made zero sense to me and I just carried on with life, trusting that guidance would come when needed.

I was a seeker of truth, light, and love. Admittedly, I was also still interested in fashion. The two did not seem to match well, but I thought I'd make it work until I'd accumulated enough money to dedicate myself fully to my spiritual endeavours.

I recall those fateful days in Paris when Spirit stopped me right in my tracks.

Nothing Is The Same After Awaking, right? James Redfield's book woke me out of my safe and predictable world, but I had to consciously choose and exert my free will to step out of the confinement of my conditioning. Once your consciousness expands beyond what society tells us we must do and be, nothing is the same anymore. We cannot undo the awakening, and life becomes our responsibility; we gain the power of Free Will.

"Do the best you can until you know better.Then when you know better, do better."

~ Maya Angelou

It takes great inner strength to do so because, all of a sudden, there are no more outside sources of power and knowing that we can trust. We only have our inner compass. Yet it is so very easy to slip back into what we have been programmed to do.

In the work that I now do with my clients, I see how tough it can be for them to exert their free will and choose the guidance of their inner compasses over that of their conditioning. I mostly midwife them through the experience and act as their strength giver, especially when they are the only ones in their family, or current reality who have awoken, which is most often the case, adding to the challenge.

Having gone through my own experience, I know just how difficult and confusing it can be to keep a clear head. Often it feels like the twilight zone. The outer reality and our conditioned minds show us one thing, but in our hearts and consciousness, there is a very different knowing that there is more—a quiet but essential voice asking to be listened to, even when it makes no sense to the conditioned mind.

How do we develop the inner strength to choose the guidance of our internal compass consistently? It's a muscle that we slowly train by sometimes getting it wrong and learning discernment. There really is no other magical way.

We must be compassionate towards ourselves and realise that just being willing to sit still with this inner conflict is already a great testimony of our inner strength.

Whenever I've listened to my inner guidance, which I see as the same as Spirit's guidance, I have been rewarded with expansion and beautiful experiences that have added to my growth. Whenever I have made choices from fear or obligation, rather than love and joy, there has been a lack of flow and comfort.

As we become better at reading the feedback from the world, from the vantage point of a neutral mind — when we learn to really feel what we are truly feeling instead of what we have been conditioned to feel — then the guidance of Spirit becomes our primary feedback mechanism.

Trust What You Feel and trust what feels good, loving, and expansive. This can be tricky; only because our conditioning would have left us with some deep wounding, which typically occur during our early childhood and leaves us feeling less thanworthy and incapable of anything.

That is probably one of the most confusing parts of learning to fully step into your purpose and power.

Looking back, I know that my stint in fashion was not actually Spirit-led, nor was it my full heart's desire. This is why it didn't work out, and why it made me sick, literally.

Like so many, I grew up in a family that prized doing over being, and only praised me for being good versus being myself. At the age of 11, I went to boarding school, where I was surrounded by the super-wealthy. I felt out of place because I did not have all the designer clothing, or the style to impress. The wound of 'not-good-enough' flourished in me, and began driving my every action and obfuscated my judgment, making it difficult for me to discern what my real desires and truth were.

Therefore, while I followed Spirit's guidance to move to South Africa, I did not immediately listen to the full message. I only listened partially, and yet that experience was very much a part of my healing. When I was offered the opportunity to be the creative director for this fashion brand, there were many warning signs, as things did not flow smoothly with the owners and things did not feel good. I was not honoring my Spirit.

Taking this position allowed me to experience being good enough. Even if it was not in full alignment, it allowed me to heal the wound of having missed out in my earlier years and to complete a soul that was yearning, only to see that I did not care about fashion at all.

The Sacred Wound is the entry point for Spirit's guidance to work in us. If we are to grow, evolve, and become masters of our own lives, we must incur the sacred wound and see just how soul-destroying it is to live from that point. Most of us will do anything possible to not expose the holy wound. We'll cover it up in shame, numb ourselves, create repeating drama patterns, and make ourselves sick.

Please understand that it takes enormous strength to allow and trust ourselves to feel *All* of our feelings without judgment. Only those with deep inner strength will be able to hold all of themselves with loving-kindness, with an all-encompassing knowing that resonates with their souls.

I had a client who had been suffering from bulimia her whole life. She could not understand why she was trapped in this destructive pattern until we uncovered that she felt very shameful for wanting so much more from life than her mother had been allowed. She had been called selfish and egotistical since she was a little girl, which led her to grow up believing that what she desired was too much, too selfish, inappropriate. Yet her soul's yearning could not be suppressed, and the only way she could feel like she was serving herself was to binge and purge.

She saw how her eating habits were a substitute for wanting to be entirely herself. Consuming a large amount of food gave her a sense of control and satisfaction that she could not otherwise get. The purging was a result of the enormous shame and guilt she felt for having these selfish desires to be herself in the first place.

Only through feeling all the feelings and contemplating her actions from a neutral mind could she begin to love herself enough to accept and love her bulimia. This then led her to accept and love herself fully.

As Rachel began to honor her true desires and step into her creativity and power, the bulimia naturally ceased to have a reason for being. Her sacred wound led to her liberation, as it always does when we embrace the perfection of everything.

That fateful and dramatic day in Paris when I fell, needed to happen. I needed things to get that bad before I could receive the message, before I could be ready to take action.

Hitting rock bottom was the best thing that could have ever happened to me, because it forced me to come face to face with everything.

I was out of excuses and I was finally too weak to run away from my situation. I had to contend with my sick and worn-out body. I had to sit with the truth that my job was not fulfilling. I had to be with my discomfort of sending my children to school. I had to face the fact that I wanted more out of my marriage and life. I had to admit that I was not yet fully healed. I had to admit that I wasn't excited about my life the way it was.

It was hard to face it all at once, especially since it felt like I had already done everything that I needed to do.

The first step was just sitting with the truth of it all and trusting that everything was still going according to plan, trusting that my dis-ease was just me being out of alignment with my own truth.

I am not suggesting that it's easy. It's not easy. It requires all of our inner strength to trust life so thoroughly that we even trust the suffering it brings us.

My client, Maria, was an excellent example of being out of alignment and suffering for it, especially when yet another relationship ended. There are wounds caused by past traumas. Her abandonment wound was causing her to spiral out of control, and this brought on utter exhaustion.

It wasn't until she could see that she was playing out her childhood all over again that she could start to heal. Her abusive father was not emotionally available to her, so she internalized the abuse and learned that she could not trust others. She was choosing men who would not fully commit to her. She had not experienced stable, nurturing love.

In her psyche, love equaled abuse and instability. It wasn't until she was able to understand and observe those patterns that she was able to realise why she kept being abandoned; she was choosing men who were not capable of being there for her. She did not know that her pain was trying to point her towards the missing alignment. The balancing of her alignment came when she realized that she was not at fault for her father's inability to love her.

The lack of her father's love did not mean that Maria was wrong or unworthy; it was merely his deep wounding that made him unable to be present for his daughter. Once Maria understood those points, she could let go of her feelings of shame and guilt, the anguish she felt for not having been loved by her father. She could then feel compassion for him and for herself. This new understanding allowed Maria to heal her wound of unworthiness and to fully step into her feminine power. Like a domino effect, this allowed her to attract her dream partner within six months of practicing a ritual we created for her.

Would she have been able to overcome her wounds and heal without continued suffering and experiencing even more abandonment by abusive men who were not able to provide the level of comfort and support that she genuinely desired? We were certain that, in the state she was in, she would not have been able to achieve this; not without support.

She needed the tools to overcome this cycle. She had to hit rock bottom and fall into despair before she could finally find the motivation to break the spell, before she could finally recognise that this was a cycle she could not continue in. Maria had to own her desire to be loved fully by a man that would be committed and available to her. She realized that she hadn't allowed herself to hold and claim that desire because she thought she wasn't worthy of a man that was committed.

Once she was able to see her suffering as a gift, she could then feel gratitude for the last man who had abandoned her.Once she owned her desire for a soul mate, her soul mate showed up, like magic. She was finally ready to be with a man that loved and adored her wholeheartedly. Accepting this love wasn't easy in the initial stages of the relationship, because she was still overcoming the belief that love was equal to abandonment. Yet, her new partner's love slowly healed her wounded heart and matured her into a woman that was standing unapologetically in her own power.

When I came home from Paris, my body crashed. I had, kind of seen it coming but before my fashion stint. My energy started dwindling daily, my digestion was completely off, I was bloated, puffy, sore; nothing digested. I could not sleep at night and had night terrors but was totally exhausted in the day. My brain fog got so bad that I could not think straight nor read, and I just felt like I was losing it. Migraines were a monthly occurrence and my body was in constant pain.

Eventually, after months of wrong diagnosis I was diagnosed with severe adrenal fatigue, hashimotos (an autoimmune dis-ease) and fibromyalgia. No doctor could really offer me a secure healing path; only a bunch of supplements and pills which did nothing but make me feel worse.

I had 20 years of nutritional studies under my belt, including time spent in India studying Ayurveda under a master, and I thought I knew everything about health. I stabbed around in the dark for several months trying out various healing modalities and diets but nothing seemed to work. By then, I was reacting to everything.

My body would swell; I had brain fog to the point where even reading was challenging. Getting up to go to the bathroom took as much energy as a massive hike in a snow storm and my little children kept asking me, "why are you always in bed mama?"

I was terrified. During the day, I was exhausted to the point where three naps were not enough. At night, I was wired for hours and could not sleep.

I was convinced I had some mystery illness and that I was on my way out.

I started researching as much as I could, and one day I stumbled upon teachings around dry fasting (no food and no water for periods at a time), juice fasting and *TheMucusless Diet Healing System.*

It all seemed so far out, but somehow my soul was deeply resonating with all this information. As much as I was terrified to go through with it, I had no other choice. I dove into a 40 day fast of just grape juice and herbal tinctures (called The Master Fast System); I was sold from my first round and whilst initially I got worse, I could feel that this was the way. Over the next two and a half years, I completed seven rounds of 40 days fasting and in between applied the teachings from Dr. Arnold Ehret, and other natural hygienists like Dr. Jensen, Dr. Morse, Dr. Sebi, Dr. Fred Bisci and various other experts in the field.

As crazy and radical as it all seemed, my body and soul were responding like never before. I slowly began to not only heal, but also felt better than I had ever remembered feeling. I was receiving powerful guidance from Spirit consistently as to what I needed to do next and I incorporated the deep spiritual work along with the physical healing. This gave me the understanding that everything I thought I was doing before was child's play, This Was The Real Deal. It was hardcore, but the results were incredible.

My body healed and rejuvenated visibly beyond what I thought was possible, but the most powerful transformation was on a soul and personal level. My whole life I had lived with depression, life was hard and I had come to just make peace with it. Now I was totally transformed. My lingering depression was totally lifted, and I became filled with light and inspiration. It felt like someone had finally turned the lights on!

Part of me didn't want to believe it; I even had moments where I thought I was going crazy, but the results were undeniable. My whole being became filled with joy and the light of God. I felt a constant stream of connection to source and it was as if my lifebecame guided by God's hand. Cleaning out my body of old accumulated waste and acid forming foods proved to be life changing. It was exactly as all the books I read had described. I had incredibly deep insights around the nature of disease, and how our addictions to the wrong foods were keeping our spirit stunted, and our bodies sick.

I started to share my findings and experiences on social media out of a genuine desire to share and inspire, and things just started taking off like wildfire.

Before I knew it, I had a global following; people were writing me and even calling from all parts of the world to share how deeply my teachings were impacting their lives.

Before I knew it, I was coaching clients worldwide and people were healing from ailments that they could not heal from.

I finally felt I was home... I knew this was my purpose. I had known from the age of five that I was here to shed light on the true nature of dis-ease. Back then, I was obsessed with my parent's encyclopedia on health and dis-eases and would secretly go and look through that book whenever I could.

I realized that for years I had disowned my gift as a healer. As the results were rolling in and people started to heal from the impossible, even cancer, I could no longer deny that I was here to guide others into a whole new way of living.

I evolved the fasting and 'mucusless' diet healing system of Dr. Ehret and combined it with deep inner work that would allow people to heal their deepest inner wounds and step into their highest purpose.

What I repeatedly observed and learned was that when we consume foods that are mucus forming and stimulating, not only does our body suffer, but our soul also becomes clouded due to weakness in our endocrine system, which results in our severance from our innate connection to Source.

My own healing journey has been my university and masters degree; and working with clients has become my ongoing PhD. I remain a student of life with the knowledge that what we consume deeply affects our consciousness.

I truly feel that collectively we are at the brink of a huge evolutionary leap in consciousness and that our way of nourishing our bodies has everything to do with it.

My whole view on healing and dis-ease has radically shifted, and I am committed to inspiring people as to just how miraculous our human bodies are, and that they are the seat of consciousness.

Embodiment is the new Enlightenment. We need to fully embodying our body and learn how to use it to our full advantage.

This lifestyle has not only healed me beyond what I thought was possible, it has guided me to my life's purpose and literally given me a whole new lease on life.

My family and I now travel the world teaching and running retreats, as well as certifying practitioners; and we are about to open our first cutting edge detox retreat centre in Bali.

"Isn't it hard to live on mostly fruit and vegetables?"

That is the question I get the most and the answer is No, it is pure bliss! Especially when you feel better at 46 than when you were a teenager!

Words cannot quite describe the levels of pure bliss and ecstasy I have experienced since living this lifestyle.

The clarity of mind, the guidance of Spirit, the level of vitality and constant energycannot be put into words, and it is still improving six years into this journey... I can only say that I remain awed at this life and the perfection of nature.

It took all I had to commit to this journey, but I also feel like I wasn't given much choice and I would not change a thing. Because once you are living your soul's purpose, there are no more questions, no more desires, no more lack - just the pure bliss of knowing you are living the life you came here to live.

This does not mean it's always perfect, or what you want; just that you feel a constant yes from Spirit.

When I realised that my disease was my greatest gift and that it finally allowed me to go after everything I ever desired, I could only feel excitement. Of course, there was still fear of whether or not I would make it, but the excitement took over.

If I was going to go through the effort of healing, I also needed to recognise all of my desires. I would need to own what I wanted. Initially, it seemed all too much. I wondered how I was going to change all the things that seemed not to fit into my dream life. I was too weak to work at my dreams, and there appeared to be so much that needed fixing.

I found that fasting helped me tremendously. Initially, it seemed to make everything worse, but my soul guided me to fast so that I might better fulfill all my desires.

As I fasted, I was able to understand many of my patterns and from where they originated. Spirit also kept reassuring me that everything was perfectly arranged to be the launchpad for my most magnificent life. My inner guidance kept pointing me towards the next thing I needed to tackle. I needed to trust the process and allow my guides to work on my behalf.

My body had to come first. Fasting and detoxing became my focus, despite how difficult it sometimes was. It was difficult to love myself enough to do what I needed to do. However, I did it because I had one goal in mind, and that was to heal myself and live in my dream life.

One day the voice said, "It's time to take your children out of school." I was scared because I knew I wasn't the type of person who wanted to home school my children, but the voice said, "Trust yourself, trust your life, trust your children." Therefore, I did. I was scared and excited, and thus a new adventure began.

Step by step, I followed the instructions of Spirit. I knew I was being led into what I needed to accomplish, and felt it wise to follow what I was being told to do. From the outside, it looked like my life was falling apart and as if I were going crazy.

I lost friends and, at one point, even my parents turned away from me. It was difficult and there were moments of fear, but the exhilaration was there, too! I was creating MY dream life, and, as crazy as it seemed, I had to trust it.

I realized that I often wished so badly that I could be more normal. I wished my dreams would fit into what other people and my family seemed to find acceptable. But the truth was, what was emerging from me was a whole new vision for life. I had to trust it because it was not what I had hoped for. It was simply the Divine truth that was arising through me. I found myself trying to trust something that I was also fighting to understand.

The more I healed my body, the more I realised that most of us have been living life from a fundamentally flawed premise. We mistrust and fear life itself because we are disconnected from the source of our innate Divinity. We try so hard to avoid our pain, not realising that we cause most of it ourselves. We are ultimately causing those around us more pain because we mistrust pain. If we mistrust the process, we ultimately delay constant growth. We find it hard to see that suffering is just part of the process God/Goddess uses to point us in the right direction.

We don't own our true desires because of our wounds. We seek out substitutes that create more suffering and dis-ease. Fasting and cellular detoxification has brought me total clarity on all fronts and has allowed me to see how all suffering is human-made.

Once we give each thing its rightful place and see how we create everything for our highest evolution, then life becomes fun and suffering becomes optional. Claiming our power as creators makes an experience genuinely magical, easy and, at the same time, it brings enormous humility when we realize that All Is Connected; nothing ever lives in isolation.

There is no shame in suffering, no shame in hitting rock bottom, once we get the lessons and run with them. If you see things from that viewpoint, it makes it impossible to mess this life up.

By claiming my desires and listening to my internal guidance, I was able to heal my body and make myself a vessel for the Divine to flow through. This has guided me into creating a life that I am deeply in love with. All of it!

Everything is just as I've dreamed it would be. Yet, it is not done. It's a dream that I am continuing to imagine; a dream that gets bigger and better. Nothing is a problem anymore. There are no more questions, only answers. If something doesn't feel right, I know I simply have to come back into alignment. There is no panic or fear, just alignment.

By keeping my body clean, I remain open to being guided from Source, and that continues to be the most awe-inducing experience of my life. I know now with every cell of my being that I, like every other being on the planet, am Divine. We are here for only one purpose, and that is to shine with Divine perfection upon those that are willing to receive it. We need to celebrate this gift of life by creating what gives us joy, and to fully trust that life has our back.

"Go within everyday and find the inner strength so that the world will not blow your candle out."

~ Katherine Dunham

CHAPTER TEN

❖

The What, How,
And Why Of An Entrepreneur

By Mohammad Hisham

Hi, my name is Hisham. Entrepreneur. Coffee aficionado. Terran.

I was born and bred in a sleepy and riverine town of Sibu in East Malaysia. I come from an average middle-class Malaysian family and received tertiary education in Australia. I am among the very few who decided to return to Malaysia to contribute to the nation.

I consider myself an accidental entrepreneur. I was a drifter and just went wherever life would lead me. Upon returning to Sarawak, I applied to, and was rejected by various governmental and private sector employers twenty-six times in one year. The rejections were partly due to employers favouring non-degree holders for cheaper hire. I ended up as a tuition teacher while, at the same time, helping my father with the family businesses in building maintenance and service industries. There was not much fame, glory or money in what I did, as compared to my friends who were overseas. There was some sense of shame, and I took no pride with the business empire my father had established for himself over the decades. I did not feel like I had accomplished anything significant with my life.

It was not until I met and married my wife that I realized how deeply embedded I was in my comfort zone. Seeing how lackadaisical I was, my wife began a small home business of selling homemade pastries, while working as a government servant during the day; just to show how much an individual can do within 24 hours. You see, like most millennials, I could be categorized as someone who had never experienced hardships due to my comfortable upbringing, and I would stop trying after a few meager attempts. But after seeing how hardworking my other half was, I eventually got her point. I ventured into an entirely unknown territory; Starting a business.

However, there was a problem. I did not know what I really wanted to do.

I had many ideas at one time but was unable to implement any due to over-thinking and human limitations. I had very few ideas to put into a business at one time, and that led to losses that were preventable. I had angrily rushed to open a business because I felt my business partners were moving too slow and the ensuing squabbles about management styles caused dissolution. My lack of control of my own physical, mental, and emotional state led to the premature closures of my first three businesses.

My life was a mess, chaotic, and any other synonymous adjective you can think of.

As all of this chaos was happening, one of the businesses stuck out and survived. It was a grocery delivery startup, by which customers get their groceries delivered to their homes and offices. This concept was very alien at that time in Sibu, in 2016, and skeptics did comment that it would not gain enough traction to be a viable business. They were right, as my only regular customer was my mother-in-law and the rest were one-off buyers.

Somehow, somewhere along the line, that miniscule business turned into a food delivery service in early 2017, which was again another alien concept while the rest of the world has had it since the 2000s. Despite the critics, it did gain traction and what was once supposed to be an obscure business became a recognized startup.

It was not long before the government unexpectedly called us to fly over to the capital of Kuala Lumpur to receive the Top 31Malaysia Entrepreneur Startup award from the Ministry of Finance in December 2017. This was followed by the Startups to Watch from the Global Entrepreneurship Movement in 2018 and

Top 100 Asia Pacific Startups from e27 Echelon in 2019. And in 2020, we received grants to upgrade our business. The upgraded platform, BeGÖ, was created as an on-demand booking super platform, which provides deliveries, service bookings, and intra-city marketplace. We are now in the midst of rolling out the platform across Sarawak and eventually across the region.

You may see the growth and success of BeGÖ as the result of perseverance, strong business acumen, and luck. That is the generic successful entrepreneur attributes you can apply onto almost any established businessman today. Honestly, it was none of those. You see, I myself was, and sometimes still a hard-headed and short-fused person. I am allergic to nonsense and am someone who is not amused if you ask me out for a drink just to sell me insurance. All of this may have contributed to my naivety, cockiness, and other stereotypical millennial attributes, which ultimately led to the aforementioned failures.

Just as there are external changes you can apply to better yourself, there are also internal changes you can make which I believe a lot of us have missed nowadays. These internal changes—or specifically this inner engineering—are what I have learned and practiced over the years as an entrepreneur. In layman's terms, you have to organize your mind. Others may have shared experiences based on their industries, and thus, I am going to share the three self-applied inner engineering principles relevant to those who want to start or have started a business. The three changes: know what you want, have faith, and remind yourself why you are doing it.

Let's start with knowing what you want in life. Many of us are unhappy because life has not gone the way we wanted it to go. The problem lies within ourselves, whereby we make decisions based on compulsion and not consciousness. Whenever we see the queue to get the latest Smartphone with its super cool new features, we want to buy one for fear of being left out. Whenever we get some fast food, we casually drink sodas filled with dissolved carbon dioxide when we know our bodies need oxygen. Whenever someone hurts us emotionally or criticizes our hard work, we vow vengeance and want to show the world what we can do just to prove them wrong.

In the examples above, we can see how our wants come from our reacting to life. When other people decide where you should go, how you should eat, or what you should wear, you can call this slavery. But when people decide what should happen within you, isn't that slavery, too?

In life, people can provoke you emotionally, mentally, and physically, which may cause your life to go haywire. When your daily life is out of control, then you have almost no control of your destiny. You end up unsure of what you want in life, and you let others decide what you want in life.

If you have much control over your physical body, your mind and emotions, then you will notice how the world will start following you. Instead of becoming a slave to the situation, you create the situation you want.

Can you guess what you want by now? If you want to say you would like to get rich, to travel around the world, or to become a leader in your industry, then you are absolutely wrong.

There is a similarity in people who go to the same workplace for years; people who sit in a bar to drink, and people who go to a place of worship religiously. All these activities bring them a sense of fulfillment, pleasure, and peace.

These three feelings are what we human beings want in life or hereafter.

Once you discover what you enjoy doing the most, then you will treat your work as a hobby. A hobby is a regular activity you do for enjoyment and typically during your leisure time. And when work becomes a hobby, suddenly the concept of entrepreneurial burnout and office hours vanishes. This can be seen in many entrepreneurs such as Bill Gates, who started Microsoft in his tiny Albuquerque garage; a young Jack Ma, who purposefully became a tour guide to learn English in China before starting Alibaba, and Elon Musk, who stayed behind in his Tesla electric car factory during his birthday. I discovered mine connecting the Sarawakian community to opportunities on the internet since 2017, and the experience is fulfilling. We all love what we do regardless of where, what, and when we do it. So, when you do find something that gives you a sense of fulfillment, pleasure, and peace; commit to it. That is what you want.

The second inner engineering you can apply is to have faith. You may have heard or known someone who wants something and against all odds gets it in the end, and this usually happens to a man of faith.

You can have faith in the Divine; that voice in your head, your gut, karma, anything. This drives us internally to transform an idea into reality. It has the similar effect of a father training his child to ride a bicycle, only for the father to quietly let the child go to cycle on his own while believing his father is still supporting him.

I would like to share a story from one of my trips to Bali, Indonesia. Bali is a predominantly Hindu province in the Muslim-majority Indonesia. My tour guide, Nyoman, brought us to a traditional Hindu home during a cultural tour and explained the significance of their dailyofferings and prayers. Nyoman jokingly explained that if he prayed to God to give him a BMW, God was not going to drop a BMW from the sky and land it conveniently next to him. Nyoman still had to be a hardworking tour guide with his own effort, create savings with his own money, and walk to a BMW car dealer to purchase one with his own will and money. He could then do this comfortably knowing he had the blessing from the Divine.

This, I personally believe, is the correct basis of the majority of faiths around the world.

However, you can still do this second inner engineering wrongly. The first mistake is when you profess a belief in God or other ideologies and then let life take its course. God would not lift a finger for you because He has provided everything you need to succeed in life. Watching inspirational videos from Jack Ma will not make you the next Jack Ma if you keep sitting there watching for the next few years. You must realize how blessed you are to be alive and to have technologies to help you get started in your pursuit of success. You must take control of your life and make clear what you want to do with what has been provided for you.

The second mistake is when you think for yourself what is possible and otherwise. Faith only works for simple folks, not overly thoughtful ones. Imagine you going to a place of worship and praying to the Divine to let you start a new business successfully.

Dear God, I want to start a successful multi-billion-dollar business. But I only have $100 in my pocket and I need $100,000 to really get things started.

There is that big "But" in that sentence.

You are already telling yourself it is not possible and yet you are still asking for it, which creates confusion within yourself. This happens because we have mostly become an over-thinking species. We criticise, judge, and criticise again as the current environment today requires us to do, so we can avoid being scammed or lied to. If Jesus were to return today for his Second Coming, there is a high possibility most of us will be skeptical; share skepticism over WhatsApp, and create Facebook groups to question his legitimacy despite all the miracles he has performed. Now compare yourself to a simple man who goes to the same place of worship and prays to the Divine.

Dear God, I want to start a successful multi-billion-dollar business. I don't care how, but I know you can help me do it.

There is not a sense of negativity in that request, and that simple man will most likely succeed because no limitation exists in his mind to stop him. It is not our role to decide what is possible and impossible. Our role is to strive to get what we want and let nature decide what is possible or otherwise. So, have faith, put your limiting thoughts aside, and tell the man in the mirror he is a successful entrepreneur every single day.

We now move on to the third and final self-applied inner engineering;why are we doing it?

Entrepreneurship is not for everyone.

Let that sentence sink in for a while. Starting a business is not a glamorous endeavour, and it is not guaranteed to make you a millionaire before age 30. It is okay to admit defeat and leave if this path is not for you. It is also okay to keep on failing ten times, learning ten times from said failures, and to finally rise up on the 11th attempt.

However, the chronic stress from making decisions, handling problems, and making sureeveryone gets paid each month can take a toll on people. Imagine experiencing all that stress every day for the next five years until you question the point of continuing. This is called Entrepreneurial burnout. Entrepreneurial burnout is a common and visible problem in many startups and even in veteran businessmen, and it is nothing to be ashamed about. To simply counter the burnout, you will just need to remind yourself why you are on this entrepreneurial path with the following sentence:

Whatever kind of business you are into, there is only one business; human well-being.

There have been so many types of industries and businesses in existence for the last 100 years, but some did not survive due to obsolescence. For example, the diskette industry which helps produce storage to save 100 KB worth of files has become obsolete and only remains as 'Save As' icons in many computers today. Bakery and other similar food industries remain relatively unchanged during the last decade, as food is a basic human necessity. From these comparisons, we can see that a business can survive if it addresses the human needs. I personally believe the only business which will survive the next 100 years will be the ones involving human well-being.

I have seen many startups die or thrive over the past few years. I do admire unicorns, a term for businesses under five years old with a valuation of $1 billion, and how they have changed the lives of their communities for the better. I have also seen distasteful decisions made at the expense of the people. As much as profit is the main indicator of how successful a startup is, the number of people's lives you have touched and how far your operations run are other indicators you can use for references as to why you must keep on going.

You can quickly go over *YouTube*, *Netflix*, or other streaming service providers and watch *Shark Tank* or *Dragon's Den* to see entrepreneurs trying to woo investors to help them out in terms of advice or finance. After a few episodes, you can quickly see a pattern of which business may last another ten years, and which has ridiculous ideas and may close down shortly after the show. Spotting the successes and the flops is a skill you yourself, as an entrepreneur, must experience and hone in order to decide what you can do with your business. I can give a tip whereby you can take note of the types of businesses that have been around for ten years and have yet to receive any profit and compare them to one-year-old companies with fast-growth and valuation of over $2 million. It is these: businesses that solve problems can grow, but businesses, which help with human well-being, can last as long as humans exist.

When you are developing your business model, always remember to include how it can benefit the people around you. When you are stuck in a rut or a burnout, remember how many lives you've touched with your business. When you are finally successful, remember to give back to society with gratitude for supporting you all those times. With these at the back of your mind, you as an entrepreneur can and will survive a burnout or even thrive in stressful situations only to come out on top.

My journey has not ended, and I believe I still have a lot to experience in this entrepreneurial path. I admit there is still a lot of self-applied inner engineering I need to do in order to be a better businessman, a better husband, a better son, and a better human as a whole, because—let us be realistic—nobody is perfect all the time. But to strive to be perfect is perfection itself. I do feel fulfilled, and I enjoy writing and sharing my humble story with you, whether you are a budding entrepreneur or a reader who wants to know how a startup strives and thrives.

I hope to see fellow entrepreneurs, not only in Southeast Asia, but in the whole world, rise up and inspire the next generation to achieve even greater accomplishments. Making this world a better place is our responsibility, as we do not own it and are merely borrowing it from our children.

Before I conclude, I must break the fourth wall and say thank you to John Spender and his team for the opportunity to be in this book. Moreover, to live up to what I have preached, I was not happy with the previous submission and felt I could do better. This chapter was prepared overnight within four hours with intermittent sleep in between bouts of writing. I believed and had a clear vision of doing this, which I do hope is much more organized and thoughtful for you, dear readers.

All the best and I hope to see everyone at the top!

"Never trust your fears.
They don't know your
strength."

~ Athena Singh

CHAPTER ELEVEN

❖

Beyond ME

By Zeina Yazbek

Here I am today, feeling the most powerless I have ever felt.

Yet, it is my inner strength that is keeping me afloat and trusting openly.

For as long as I can remember, I've seen myself as different. I would always look at the world around me as the outside; similar to looking at a stage or a film set. "Oh! That's how *they* do it *there*," the unengaged self-narrator would say.

I am unsure as to why this remembrance is making its way to the beginning of what I am writing, but I am flowing with it and trusting that this is already part of the chapter. While every voice in my head is telling me to stop, reread and reconsider, I am finding myself going faster as if these words are only being typed by me but not written. I am seeing my fingers racing through the keyboard in anticipation, witnessing every stroke, and watching how my hands are stumbling upon each button in denial, as if someone else has taken command; someone who knows what is being said and is going a little too quickly for my hands. This someone also knows that there will come a time when I will reread this and fix what needs to be fixed.

But, just for now, I want to type without knowing.

"What is it that *you* want to type now?" My mind asks just after I've scanned through what has already been written.

My mind hits the brakes. It starts a revolution of its own. It is judging what I am doing as nonsense. It is my worse critic as it stands there tapping its feet, waiting for me to stop and ask, "Now what finally?"

I am still running with someone who is *freely* writing as I ask, "Who are you? How have you inhabited my fingers as if they were always yours and I am a visitor?"

This someone is simultaneously speaking to my mind: "I do see your value as you will help me dot the I's and cross the T's when the time comes. But for now, I am." As I type up these very words, my heart cracks open. I never knew I could breathe with my heart. It feels like an inhale without an exhale, as if my heart can absorb just about anything, no matter the size or condition. In this moment—just for a moment—I feel what it feels like to feel more like ME.

Oh, here it is. It has just happened again. My heart has widened.

ME! ME! ME! Me!

Whoa! Has it always been this easy?

Let me try again.

ME!

How come? I have never noticed that I relate more to the ME who is typing faster than my mind could process than to the ME I live with every day.

Not only is my heart still taking deep breaths now, but it also has its voice and frequency. It is a loud pitch that I have never sensed before—like a warm embrace.

"What are you doing typing this much and this fast? Why won't you write something usable, poetic, and philosophical, something with a plot twist and a rhyming meter?"

Is ME my mind's mind, or is ME a different channel? And if the latter is the case, have I been running on the wrong channel my entire life?

This person writing feels similar to the channels I tap into when I allow my imagination to weave away its world or when I watch my favorite childhood movies. Where has she been? Why am I now feeling connected to her? Does this mean that I have been *disconnected* all along?

Can I disconnect from ME? Why is this even a function?

As I keep typing, I feel as if I am in a race with myself, not against — a race of no destination, prize, end goal, or shape. I am just running fast because I can. And this race seems unfair, to be honest. I am WAY faster than my mind. It's almost like a joke.

Like Mr. Rabbit from *Alice in Wonderland*, who is always running late: *I am late. I can't stop. My house might have been taken over by a giant, but I cannot stop. I am late*, and Alice just has to follow. Late for what? Who is this rabbit who speaks and has a watch? It doesn't matter. She has to go, too.

I must keep going. The possibilities feel endless.

Endless? All of a sudden, I feel anxious, overwhelmed, and tired.

Now I want to stop.

What if I can't trace my way back from where I started? What if ME and I can't find each other again tomorrow?

Maybe I should have stayed with my mind. This endless-possibilities business is breath-stopping and heart-palpitating.

I don't know.

I don't want to think. I just want to type. I don't want a plan or software to check if I am repeating myself.

Of course, I am repeating myself, but each time is different from the one before.

Would this still make it a repetition?

Maybe repetition doesn't mean saying the *same* thing over and over. If so, it would be called the same.

One would only guess. Sometimes I feel like I am stuck in a vocabulary that just doesn't get me.

Where was I?

Oh, back here, or forward.

Whatever.

My mind is so noisy that it just went silent.

It's like a writer's brain freeze where I usually just watch the cursor: But I am not.

This time I am writing about it.

ME is going with this as the open space for anything: Type; Dance; Laugh; Kiss; Write gibberish. I don't have to make sense. I am free.

My mind is back in gear: "Who wants to hear the internal diary of you losing it?"

Not today, mind. Not now. I love you and I thank you. Here is hot chocolate for you. I have a rocket to catch.

My hands are typing too fast for me now, but I am enjoying every stroke. Breaking my own rules feels awesome. YAY! Woohoo! I can do whatever I want. I can type whatever I want because I am ME, now, in this moment, and on this very keystroke.

My own rules? I have those?

And here I thought I was a rebel.

Feeling overwhelmed, I want to stop.

Or is it my mind playing tricks on me again?

There has always been a silent but subtle voice inside of me who tells me that I willalways do ME in the end. I never knew what that meant. I still don't. Why does it have to be ME at the end?

The end of what anyway?

Blank.

Here I am, weeks later, attempting to pick this up again. I am reading through while taking almost no breaths and feeling anxious. I don't know what to write from here.

I am suffocating at the thought of not finishing this chapter on time.

I am also losing my mind.

All these hours of meditation and other different practices to silence the mind, and this is how I lose it.

My mind just called me crazy.

If I truly speak my mind without using my mind, then I am crazy. How about when I was a baby?

Were my original factory settings tuned in at *crazy*? How come no one calls babies crazy but consider them curious when they do things they're not supposed to do?

A surge of feelings just came rushing through me, along with memories of my childhood. Random visuals of the girl who was expected to be someone other than herself just started flashing before me. The child wasn't given room to be herself because she was always too much or too little. She was told she needed to *learn*. "You cannot do this," teachers would say. "You can't do that," parents would add. "You should do this," friends would whisper. My music teacher asks me to express myself while the religion instructor kicks me out for asking a question.

More memories are gushing through. One of my parents is expecting me to excel in pretty much everything, so I push. Friends are calling me nerd, so I rebel. Society wants me to be a good girl, so I pretend. The man who abused me at five years of age tells me not to say a thing or risk being judged as bad, so I lie and shame myself. Civil war forces me to numb my feelings, to build a world of illusion and division, as well as disassociate.

Meet the class president clown, the tomboyish girly girl, and everything in between.

Wow.

Anger, anguish, hurt, grief, pain...all just now comes surging along. It isn't until I dive into meditation, breath work, astrology, and other forms of inner work that all of these feelings start moving into my awareness. It is then that I realized the seed of avoiding pain and seeking pleasure that has been planted within me. Someone somehow has instilled a belief that *normal* means always to be happy and ready to do more daily. My natural lifelong response has been to judge anyone else's feelings as invalid or inhuman, and make them go away ASAP. It doesn't matter how.

No wonder I've felt a split my entire life, and by split, I don't mean just into two. There is a bunch of us here. Each one comes out to play depending on the context, environment, and level of fear of rejection.

Another remembrance is making itself written into this chapter.

I wonder why.

My 33rd birthday was the lowest I had ever felt, and the sickest I had ever experienced. The moment I decided to give myself a vacation after years of no breaks, the island doors of Bali opened to me. Little did I know, I was being given a raw dose of reality. Three days into my trip to the city of Ubud, the perfect child was ready to leave. I could no longer do it all. I couldn't plan a multi-million-dollar business campaign, finish clients' development plans, fight anxiety, remember to eat, pretend that mypersonal life isn't shit, deal with the fact that my toxic friendships weren't there, tolerate the misery of the mysterious physical pain, and *be* on vacation all at the same time.

For the first time, I found myself saying, "I will not do this anymore."

Though in denial, I knew I was going to stop. My mind launched its peak resistance. It was throwing every possible scenario at me. It felt as though the sun and moon would no longer light up the skies if I stopped pretending that I was perfectly fine andperfectly perfect.

As my thoughts were most scattered, I was able to see that my only lifeline was the death of *me*.

So, I jumped into the unknown.

The most unlikely scenario happened—the one where my mind couldn't have been farther from thinking at the time. It turns out that I have wings to carry me. Just like a bird who is learning that she was made to fly all along, I jumped, fell at times, got stuck in the mud, got lost, rested, soared, and fell again, repeatedly.

What a messy, magical being a human is.

I had been calling to ME to answer back all along. My self-conversation was so muted that it had just taken the form of a very intense physical pain, depression, insomnia...and a plane ticket.

Then, there was light. Right here within me, there was and still is so much to see and observe.

"What exactly did you observe?" my mind asked.

Ah! Form! Another seed planted within. A belief that everything should have a specific shape or be in a certain way. It was a trick of the beautiful mind that had taken me away from tapping into limitless amounts of possibilities that are already happening within and without.

This is the fixed-form curse of how I should be, how a relationship should look, and what a "good" job is— as if everything is a destination and that, once you're there, you should stay there. It sounds like a mix of death and a human cloning factory to me.

It is right here in the formless and shape-shifting flow that I found ME, and I looked like infinity.

All it took was an initiated Self-conversation.

My mind just offered a standing ovation with sarcasm.

"Very poetic. Good read. Here is a side note though: who do you think you are? "

As I contemplate the beauty and power of the mind, my mind's mind is still writing while I observe.

The self-conversation is what I had found myself introducing into my life. It began as something like this:

"As above, so below. As within, so without. As the universe, so the soul."

A saying by Hermes Trismegistus has singlehandedly reminded me of my strength. Though, at first, I thought that the very sentence meant that all is connected. I then realized that this is a suggestion of oneness, and not a smile or cause and effect. My inner world is one with my external world. My outer world is at one with my internal world. And just as there's a universe outside, there is also my soul within.

If my body is speaking to me through pain, then I can talk to my body as well.

I ask myself how I am feeling now. Then I quickly scan my body to see if any emotion is lurking about and causing back pain, neck soreness, or an anxious solar plexus. Sometimes I check in minutes later or a day later, and observe whether anything has changed or moved. I ask, "Does this feeling bring up a memory or story? Does it remind me of someone? Is it old or new?" And I make the conversation however short or long I want or need it be so that I can gain a deeper understanding as I observe. Ever since I first initiated the self-conversation, I have witnessed so much more creator, and so much more human. The observation of ME has been introduced to my built-in camera. This is the ME who knows that there is no such thing as the same forever after, or the same till-death-do-us-part, though all things are always possible. The ME who knows nothing and everything. The ME who is within me but is not I.

During restless days, I observe my mind is loud. On quiet days, I witness silence. In moments of confusion, I watch resistance and self-judgment. And this is not about being good or feeling better or anything. It's just me, myself, and I exploring the vastness or tightness of my humanness—the wonders of this spirit and physical body in the lowest of lows and highest of highs. Some days, all I can do is observe that I am unable to be in observance.

This is me today. This is me now, because ME on the next breath might change.

This is my meditation practice today.

My observed self-conversation opens the space for me to be with the flower as it's falling apart, to go into the depths, and then to blossom upward to kiss the heavens. It has allowed me to be with my emotions, as I see that there is no darkness without light, no wholeness without heartbreak, no clarity without confusion, as the pendulum of my humanness swings from one side to another and touches everything in between.

The observer has no form, no senses, but exists in all senses.

Starting the self-conversation has un-caged feelings of pain and joy, life and death, breakups and unions. And though some days it can feel heavy like a dark journey of the soul, I can simultaneously also be floating where the sun and moon still light up the skies.

I love my mind, even though he mostly drives me up the wall. I gift him infinity daily. Every time I think that I am cornered in a choice, or stuck or numb, I acknowledge my mind's scenarios and I introduce the question: What if?

Yes, mind. This surely can happen, and so can that; but what if infinity can also happen?

What if?

And I close my eyes allow myself to imagine.

What a blessing this has been. It is tapping into infinity, and what it brings through the gates of endless possibilities that have stretched open the gates of the seen and the unseen.

In my heaviest and darkest days, and in my most beautiful inspiring moments, there is a universe within me, revealing itself to me one breath at a time.

All I need to do is connect and say, sure, but what if? Because infinity is just like me: endless.

And when you want to remember how strong you are…

Close your eyes as you open your sight…

Observe the self-conversation…

Imagine.

"It is worth remembering that the time of greatest gain in terms of wisdom and inner strength is often that of greatest difficultly."

~ Dalai Lama

Author Biographies

❖

John Spender

CHAPTER ONE

Iohn Spender is a 19-time International Best Selling co-author, who didn't learn how to read and write at a basic level until he was ten years old. He has since traveled the world, and started many businesses leading him to create the best-selling book series, *A Journey Of Riches*. He is an Award Winning International Speaker and Movie Maker.

John was an international NLP trainer and has coached thousands of people from various backgrounds through all sorts of challenges. From the borderline homeless to very wealthy individuals, he has helped many people to get in touch with their truth to create a life on their terms.

John's search for answers to living a fulfilling life has taken him to work with Native American Indians in the Hills of San Diego, the forests of Madagascar, and swimming with humpback whales in Tonga, exploring the Okavango Delta of Botswana and the Great Wall of China. He's traveled from Chile to Slovakia, Hungary to the Solomon Islands, the mountains of Italy and the streets of Mexico.

Everywhere his journey has taken him, John has discovered a hunger among people to find a new way to live, with a yearning for freedom of expression. His belief that everyone has a book in them was born.

He is now a writing coach having worked with more than 200 authors from 40 different countries for *A Journey of Riches* series http://ajourneyofriches.com/ and his publishing house, Motion Media International has published 20 non-fiction titles to date.

He also co-wrote and produced the movie documentary, *Adversity,* starring Jack Canfield, Rev. Micheal Bernard Beckwith, Dr. John Demartini and many more, coming soon in 2020. Moreover, you can bet there will be a best-selling book to follow!

Susanne Zavelle

CHAPTER TWO

Susanne Zavelle was born in 1967 in Austin, Texas, but relocated to South Carolina in 1998, where she raised her family of two boys. She obtained her Bachelor of Science degree in Nursing from Texas Woman's University and worked as a Labor & Delivery nurse for many years.

Susanne is a former professional master's bikini athlete, having won 2nd place at Nationals in 2014. She went on to become an official athlete of an international Multilevel Marketing (MLM) nutrition company, and became a 6-figure earner with the same company.

In 2018, She made a move to a new start-up MLM, and earned over 1M USD in her first two years with that company. She sits on the Executive Board of She Beverages Inc. in Los Angeles and is the co-founder of a company in Santa Barbara, CA. Her hobbies include traveling, scuba diving, and staying physically fit.

Dean K Walsh

CHAPTER THREE

Fighting his way back from years of chronic pain and the accompanying emotional hardship, gave Dean Walsh, an elite athlete, the skills to flourish as a new man. Reframing meditation as 'weightlifting for the mind', and a neural workout rather than spiritual exercise, raised his threshold for managing emotional and physical pain.

What started out as a journey of destructive behaviour, turned into triumph as he cracked the code to master his mind, to find his inner strengths.

With a strong belief in the power of new beginnings, Dean relocated to Bali to create Brothers Global Adventures. Leading Retreats and Adventure

Tourism, he teaches men to reconnect to nature and the core elements within themselves that make them proud and powerful - whilst having a hell of a lot of fun. Calling on his 15 years of 'weight lifting' meditation experience, Dean also conducts Brain Training via private online coaching. For more information visit https://brothersglobaladventures.com/

Melanie Tan

CHAPTER FOUR

Melanie left the corporate world in 2009 and went in search of a life that she would love to live. That took her on an adventure of self-realization, healing and thriving.

Today, she lives the life of her dreams. Melanie is a 2x SEA Games Silver medalist in wakeboarding. She is a mature athlete, competing with girls half her age. She is also a wakeboarding and yoga instructor and a lifestyle coach, specialising in healing fast from hurt and injury.

Melanie shares her extensive experience in recovery in the hope that others can come out of pain and live a more fulfilling life. If you or someone you know is looking for a positive change to achieve more in life in a shorter time, contact Mel for a no-obligation chat. Learn more at <u>mindbodyunite.com</u>

George Kaponay

CHAPTER FIVE

After more than 15 years of working high-pressure jobs in the IT industry, George realised he was not living a meaningful, fulfilling life. In fact, he was not living at all, but only merely existing and acting out of fear, while committing himself to pursuits that drained him to the point of burnout and sickness.

Twelve years ago, all of that changed, as George and his wife Bobi, along with their twin boy/girl children, chose to listen to their intuition. Their collective sense of curiosity for learning and adventure became their future. Letting go of perceived societal norms, they took a leap of faith into a journey that changed the trajectory of their lives.

They have been to more than 50 countries and six continents. Their in the moment, inspiration-led journey of learning continues today, and allows them to live, learn and contribute to the people, cultures, places and communities they visit and live in.

George and his family now choose to live a life that's true for them. They co-create spaces of learning, adventure, exploration and possibilities where families can dream into existence their own family story and ventures. They share this through their family businesses, At Home In The World Family Retreats, The Intuition Game, Museley - The Muse for Your Family, and Destinator Travel & Dreamtime Traveler.

Richard Ayling

CHAPTER SIX

R ichard Ayling is an entrepreneur and transformational coach, with over twelve years' experience in training and personal development.

After successfully overcoming an autoimmune disease by mastering the mind-body connection and cultivating a resilience mindset, he is now driven to help people take control of their physical and mental health, and live a life of meaning and fulfilment.

In 2017, he founded Re-Align, developing a framework for both body and mind that combines powerfully grounding embodiment practices with personal development programs and coaching. He empowers individuals to find connection and growth in a strictly no-fluff, authentic and relatable way.

With over 30,000 hours of training experience in three different industries, he speaks worldwide on balancing productivity, purpose, fulfillment and flow.

When he isn't coaching or facilitating, you can find him in the surf on the mat, or learning something new with a good coffee in hand.

Andre Messina

CHAPTER SEVEN

Andre was born in Auckland N.Z. in 1967. She completed High School in 1985. She worked as a receptionist in South Auckland until she was 18 years old, and then relocated to Sydney Australia.

Here she worked as a Secretary for a Legal Firm for some time, before moving to Brisbane QLD, where she would marry a local lad, and gave birth to her three children, Nathan 25, Teigan, 22, and Riley, 19.

When her marriage broke up in 2001, she took the opportunity to delve into herself, and start a healing process that continues till today.

She currently lives on a 2000 acre property in the Northern Tablelands of NSW with her best friends Jan,

David, Carolina, and Jordan. Now, 'Uncle Lewis' from Bundjalung mob has joined her in her amazing lifestyle.

She oversees an animal sanctuary, and has many animal friends on the property. Her latest canine friend is 'Shanti', a Pomeranian x Chihuahua; her favourite cat is Kanyini, a black cat with a ragdoll mother 'Lotus,' and his father is the wild black cat of the forest!

Eric Tan

CHAPTER EIGHT

Eric Tan is a Financial Services Consultant in one of the biggest companies in Singapore. He is a Distinguished Toastmaster in Toastmasters International District 80 (Singapore).

He has conducted workshops on Leadership, Communication and Wealth Management for various multi-national companies and events in Singapore.

He passionately believes that you develop inner strength through having a fighting spirit, as well as appreciating life and the power of giving.

Alexandra Cousins

CHAPTER NINE

Alex's passion has always been in health and human optimisation. From the age of five, she was obsessed with finding out what was the source of disease. Her own health struggles drove her to study Ayurveda in India in her early 20's, where she was initiated into a high level of natural healing.

Alex's path later went deeper into nutritional studies with various healers and teachers, whilst consulting to some of the most prestigious Spas in the world; but somehow, the deeper answers she was seeking still eluded her.

She took a break from working in the healing arts, and dove into high fashion for a few years before the radical breakdown of her own health took her back into healing; but this time from a completely new perspective.

 It took her deepest health crisis to bring it all together, and initiate Alex into a whole new way of looking at health and life in a body. One of the truest healers of her time who fully embodies her teachings, Alex has most often been described due to her 360-degree approach to healing our lives on all levels.

Mohammed Hisham

CHAPTER TEN

Mohammed Hisham Khairul Nasir is a the Managing Director of Solaku from Sarawak in East Malaysia. Hisham manages the Sarawakian startup, which intends to modernize Sarawak via internet and digital economy.

He is Master of Science (Project Management) graduate from Curtin University, and is one of the technopreneurs recognized by the Sarawakian and Malaysian governments, for actively improving lives and generating jobs in line with the Industrial Revolution 4.0.

Hisham is a firm believer of effort and equity in societal development, and goes with the mantra "If you're not online today, you're invisible tomorrow."

Zeina Yazbek

CHAPTER ELEVEN

Zeina is a dreamer and an achiever. She believes in the power of imagination, creation and setting your heart desires into motion to *dream your dream onward*. Zeina's career was in television production, talent management and business consultancy.

After over a decade of "a successful career," her path had other plans for her. She had then found her calling through a physical illness, which forced her to stop andreconnect to her life's calling and wildest desires. Dedicated to the ever journey of transformation, Zeina's mission is to activate change makers into their original power.

She currently resides in Bali and is the founder of Dream A New World, a soon-to-be launched platform on dreams and imagination. She is also a Shamanic Breath work facilitator, Shamanic Astrology counselor, meditation teacher, and dream-growing guide.

"Some of us think holding on
makes us strong,
but it's letting go."

~ Hermann Hesse

Afterword

I hope you enjoyed the collection of heartfelt stories, wisdom and vulnerability shared. Storytelling is the oldest form of communication, and I hope you feel inspired to take a step toward living a fulfilling life. Feel free to contact any of the authors in this book, or the other books in this series.

The proceeds of this book will go to the Bali Street Kids Project, in Denpasar, Bali. The project gives orphaned and abandoned children a home, meals and education. You can donate to this fantastic cause here: https://ykpa.org/

Other books in the series are...

Building your Dreams : A Journey of Riches, Book Nineteen
https://www.amazon.com/dp/B081KZCN5R

Liberate your Struggles : A Journey of Riches, Book Eighteen
https://www.amazon.com/dp/1925919099

In Search of Happiness : A Journey of Riches, Book Seventeen
https://www.amazon.com/dp/B07R8HMP3K

Tapping into Courage : A Journey of Riches, Book Sixteen
https://www.amazon.com/dp/B07NDCY1KY

The Power Healing : A Journey of Riches, Book Fifteen
https://www.amazon.com/dp/B07LGRJQ2S

The Way of the Entrepreneur: A Journey Of Riches, Book Fourteen
https://www.amazon.com/dp/B07KNHYR8V

Discovering Love and Gratitude: A Journey Of Riches, Book Thirteen
https://www.amazon.com/dp/B07H23Q6D1

Transformational Change: A Journey Of Riches, Book Twelve
https://www.amazon.com/dp/B07FYHMQRS

Finding Inspiration: A Journey Of Riches, Book Eleven
https://www.amazon.com/dp/B07F1LS1ZW

Building your Life from Rock Bottom: A Journey Of Riches, Book Ten
https://www.amazon.com/dp/B07CZK155Z

Transformation Calling: A Journey Of Riches, Book Nine
https://www.amazon.com/dp/B07BWQY9FB

Letting Go and Embracing the New: A Journey Of Riches, Book Eight
https://www.amazon.com/dp/B079ZKT2C2

Making Empowering Choices: A Journey Of Riches, Book Seven
https://www.amazon.com/Making-Empowering-Choices-Journey-Riches-ebook/dp/B078JXMK5V

The Benefit of Challenge: A Journey Of Riches, Book Six
https://www.amazon.com/dp/B0778S2VBD

Personal Changes: A Journey Of Riches, Book Five
https://www.amazon.com/dp/B075WCQM4N

Dealing with Changes in Life: A Journey Of Riches, Book Four
https://www.amazon.com/dp/B0716RDKK7

Making Changes: A Journey Of Riches, Book Three
https://www.amazon.com/dp/B01MYWNI5A

The Gift In Challenge: A Journey Of Riches, Book Two
https://www.amazon.com/dp/B01GBEML4G

From Darkness into the Light: A Journey Of Riches, Book One
https://www.amazon.com/dp/B018QMPHJW

Thank you to all the authors that have shared aspects of their lives in the hope that it will inspire others to live a bigger version of themselves. I heard a great saying from Jim Rohan, "You can't complain and feel grateful at the same time." At any given moment, we have a choice to either feel like a victim of life, or be connected and grateful for it. I hope this book helps you to feel grateful, and go after your dreams. For more information about contributing to the series, visit http://ajourneyofriches.com/ . Furthermore if you enjoyed reading this book, we would appreciate your review on Amazon to help get our message out to more people.

www.ingramcontent.com/pod-product-compliance
Lightning Source LLC
LaVergne TN
LVHW051458080426

835509LV00017B/1810